WELCOME

Back when I launched MoneySavingExpert.com in 2003, personal finance journalism still mostly meant newspapers writing about shares, mortgages and the occasional wacky foray into credit cards. No wonder some of my peers sniffed at me when I wrote a 'buying the cheapest DVD player' guide.

Things have moved on a long way since. Now it's mainstream to think that it's not just inflation-linked savings, but train fares, contact lenses and cashback sites that count – if something hits the pound in your pocket, then it's personal finance. Much of this attitude shift is down to the web, which has changed the game.

> Thanks to the web, people can now come together online to take on the big companies, find and swap money-saving tips and look for advice and information.

The internet has been the biggest single cause of social change and empowerment in the past 100 years. A new force of collective consumerism has arisen. Thanks to the web, people can come together online to take on the big companies, find and swap money-saving tips and look for advice and expert information.

Companies spend billions on advertising, marketing and teaching their staff to sell. Via the internet, consumers can group together to take on the corporate might. When it works, the web can be the champion of the underdog, letting you get detailed information on subjects from trustworthy sources and a feeling that you're being backed up, all at the click of a mouse.

It means people no longer feel scared or intimidated by financial information. It's an ongoing revolution that continues to provide new tools that simply couldn't have existed before, and it continues to fascinate me.

Now, if anything, the difficulty is in filtering all the information to find out what's right for you. That's what I hope my website, MoneySavingExpert.com does. However, it's a mammoth site, so on page 6 of this book you'll find a selection of my favourite tools, guides and forums. I hope you find them – and the rest of this book – useful, and continue to use the internet to save money.

Martin Lewis

From the editor

In this era of squeezed incomes and belt-tightening, it's more important than ever to save money. In this guide we show you the best ways the web can help you cut costs, from superb free software to mouth-watering discounts that you'll find only online.

We're also delighted to include some of Martin Lewis's favourite tips and tools from the renowned MoneySavingExpert.com website, which has helped millions of people save money since its launch in 2003.

Armed with all this information, I'm confident you'll be able to use the web to cut costs, find free stuff and spot bargains.

As an added bonus, you'll find 50 pages of step-by-step guide at the back of this book to help you improve your PC for free. Enjoy!

Daniel Booth
Editor

Contents

From essential free downloads to expert ways of speeding up your PC, you'll find hundreds of money-saving tricks inside

Workshops

SAVE MONEY ONLINE

EDITORIAL
Editor Daniel Booth
Production Steve Haines
Design and layout Colin Mackleworth

PHOTOGRAPHY
Danny Bird, Jan Cihak, Pat Hall,
Hugh Threlfall

MANAGEMENT
MagBook Manager Dharmesh Mistry
Digital Production Manager Nicky Baker
Production Director Robin Ryan
Managing Director John Garewal

Managing Director of Advertising
Julian Lloyd-Evans
Chief Operating Officer Brett Reynolds
Group Finance Director Ian Leggett
Chief Executive James Tye
Chairman Felix Dennis

MAGBOOK
The MagBook brand is a trademark of
Dennis Publishing Ltd.
30 Cleveland St, London W1T 4JD.
Company registered in England. All
material © Dennis Publishing Ltd,
licensed by Felden 2011, and may not be

reproduced in whole or part without the
consent of the publishers.
Save Money Online ISBN 1-907779-94-9

LICENSING
To license this product, please contact
Hannah Heagney on +44 (0) 20 7907
6134 or email hannah_heagney_@dennis.
co.uk

LIABILITY
While every care was taken during
the production of this MagBook, the
publishers cannot be held responsible

for the accuracy of the information or
any consequence arising from it. Dennis
Publishing takes no responsibility for the
companies advertising in this MagBook.
The paper used within this MagBook
is produced from sustainable fibre,
manufactured by mills with a valid
chain of custody.
Printed at BGP.

recycle

MARTIN LEWIS'S
MONEY-SAVING TIPS

Martin Lewis has become *the* champion of money-savers everywhere since launching MoneySavingExpert.com in 2003. Here he explains the best features on the site – and how they can save you money

· ·

NEWSLETTER
www.moneysavingexpert.com

Our newsletter is the core of everything we do – over 5.6 million people receive it every week. If you get the newsletter for a year and act on the things in it, you'll be giving yourself a money makeover.

We deliberately alternate stories about 'hard' and 'soft' money, so there are lots of great deals thrown in among news about serious finance. My aim is that people who don't think they're into finance might get drawn in by an appealing discount code – say 50 per cent off at Body Shop. Then they'll see they need to top up their state pension because it could save them £20,000.

TAX CODE CHECKER

www.mse.me/taxcodes

We would love to have built a checker where you enter your tax code and it tells you definitively whether you have the wrong code. We couldn't do that, but we can tell you if it's likely you have the wrong code using our Tax Code Checker.

The largest amount someone got back using Tax Code Checker was over £9,000 – absolutely massive. If you discover that you have been paying too much tax then you should read our guide to reclaiming your money, which immediately follows the Checker.

AMAZON DISCOUNT FINDER

www.mse.me/amazon-tool

The Amazon Discount Finder is about manipulating Amazon's URLs, so you can see all the products that are being discounted. You simply select your category and your discount, and it creates a page of discounts from that. We call it Amazon's hidden bargain basement.

It's a great way of finding massive discounts. If you search for 90 per cent discounts then you're picking things up for a quid or two.

PREMIUM BOND CALCULATOR

www.mse.me/premium-bonds

Our Premium Bond Calculator was incredibly hard to build because the calculations are so complex. We hired a cosmology statistician, whose job it is to work out the inter-relations of star movements – it was the only profession we could find that used that type of calculation! He built the algorithm that the calculator uses, and we then checked it with a professor of financial

mathematics at the London School of Economics to validate it.

You can use the Calculator to work out whether it's actually worth investing in Premium Bonds. Our myth-busting guide also explains the pros and cons of investing this way.

FLIGHTCHECKER

www.mse.me/flightchecker

With most flight-comparison sites, you tell them when you want to fly, and they find the cheapest fare. But with our tool, you tell it where you want to fly to, and it will tell you when to go to get the cheapest flight.

We're currently planning a massive relaunch of the FlightChecker. In the new version, you'll be able to search for any country in Europe, a beach destination, a city or a stag-do destination. You'll be able to build your own bespoke I'll-go-anywhere list.

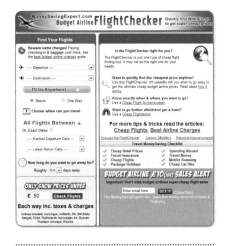

TRAVEL MONEY MAX

www.mse.me/tmm

Travel Money Max is an automated list of online currency sites. You put in how much foreign currency you want – and it includes everything, from dollars to Malaysian Ringgits. It then looks at the

rates and commission offered by sites and tells you the best deal.

If you're looking to pay for the currency to be delivered, it's worth thinking about the company you're dealing with. We have lots of information about that.

BUDGET PLANNER

www.mse.me/budgetplanner

When I wrote my first book I developed this budget plan because I looked at existing budget planners available to the public and I thought they were all rubbish. It's better than other budget planners because first, it has over 100 categories, and second, it lets you look at your spending by the week or year, not just the month. It splits everything up and does all the calculations for you.

You can get the budget planner as a spreadsheet, but there's also a hugely popular online Budget Brain version. You put in all your details and it tells you what you're spending. There's nothing else like it that's free to use.

CALLCHECKER

www.mse.me/callchecker

Most phone-comparison sites tell you what package you want. But actually to really save money you should first get your cheap package and then, depending on the call, use a different provider.

That's not as arduous as you may think, because most of these other providers are override providers, so you simply override your existing

network by dialling a different phone number. It's interesting to use this as an alternative to VoIP, which may be cheap when making internet-to-internet calls, but is more expensive when dialling internet-to-phone.

With CallChecker, you simply enter which country you want to call, and it will tell you the cheapest override provider to use. It gives you a number to call, you dial it, and you get that cheaper price.

We've upgraded CallChecker this year because we used to list just the price for dialling from BT. Now you tell it who your home phone provider is, and it will give you the price to dial the country you specified from the different companies.

It works primarily for international calls, but also if you're calling a mobile in the UK. The savings can be phenomenal, and can make your phone calls up to 95 per cent cheaper.

CAR INSURANCE JOB PICKER

www.mse.me/jobpicker

I've always called this a fun tool, because it's art, not science. It gives you an indication of how much you can save on your car insurance simply by changing your job title.

It's important to clarify that we're not recommending that you lie when you apply for car insurance. However, many people don't have a fixed job title. For example, someone could be classed as a PA, an office worker, an office assistant or a secretary. So what you can do is enter a few job titles that match what you do for a living, and see which one gives you the cheapest car insurance.

The key to what's legal is if, in court, your job title would be deemed a reasonable description of what your vocation is. If you're a secretary, and you can find much cheaper car insurance as a pig farmer, that would be illegal.

PPI RECLAIMING GUIDE

www.mse.me/ppireclaim

If you've had a credit card or loan in the past six years, you should check if you were sold Payment Protection Insurance (PPI) with it. Often you get sold PPI without realising it, which makes it hard to reclaim.

Our guide shows you how to check if you were sold PPI, and provides free template letters that you can send to lenders to ask for your money back. This approach is much better than going with one of those companies that ring you up claiming that they can get your PPI money back on a 'no win, no fee'-style basis. They take 25 per cent of your money as a commission – a fee you can avoid if you use our templates.

MENTAL HEALTH AND DEBT HELP

www.mse.me/mentalhealth

This free 40-page PDF booklet is a real passion of mine and one of the things I'm most proud of. It's supported by mental health charities Mind, Rethink, CAPUK and others, and is for people with mental health problems and those caring for them. It covers how to handle debts when you're ill, how to deal with banks, where to go for

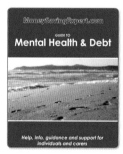

free debt counselling, tips for bipolar or depression sufferers, whether you should declare a condition and much more.

Debt can cause mental health problems, and mental health can cause debt problems – the two feed off each other. It's an increasingly common problem, and a lot of people have contacted us after reading this guide who were pleased to find they weren't suffering alone.

CAR INSURANCE GUIDE

www.mse.me/carins

We always try to take things further than price-comparison sites, and the car insurance guide shows you how to use those sites so you can get the best deal. We look at the coverage of each comparison site – because they all include different companies – and calculate how you can get the widest coverage in the shortest time.

We also tell you what you're not told on comparison sites. For example, Aviva and Direct Line aren't included on price-comparison sites, so we provide links to those companies. We also tell people that comparison sites use estimates, and advise them to double-check the details. Finally, we show you how to buy insurance through cashback sites to see how much money you can get back.

BALANCE TRANSFERS GUIDE

www.mse.me/topbts

This is what MoneySavingExpert.com is all about. Comparison sites aren't bad: they give you a list based on their specification. The problem is that most people don't know what they need.

What we do is first of all ensure that a balance transfer is the right thing for you – that choosing a 0 per cent card is what you need. Every day we manually update the cards that are available, explaining how they work. We also show you how to keep your costs down once you get your card.

STOOZING GUIDE

www.mse.me/stoozing

Stoozing is a method of cleverly manipulating credit cards so you make money. The idea is to pay for your monthly outgoings on cards offering 0 per cent interest. This means you can put an equivalent amount of money from your salary into a high-interest savings account, so you're earning interest on money they've lent you for free. Just remember to always pay off the minimum repayment every month. Our stoozing calculator will show you how much money you can save.

HOTEL TRICKS

www.mse.me/cheaphotels

One of my favourite hotel tricks involves Lastminute.com's secret hotel offer (http://bit/ly/hotel secret). You know the star rating and description of the hotel, but you don't know what the hotel is until after you've paid. But if you cut and paste the right words from the description into Google you can find out which hotel it is. Then you can really find out if you're getting a bargain by putting the hotel into a comparison site.

Even more powerful is a trick for Priceline (www.priceline.co.uk). You get to bid once in 24 hours on the price of a hotel room. You can get massive savings, but you don't know which hotel you're going to get. But what you really want to do is bid the lowest price that will be accepted, and our guide shows you a trick to do that.

I should mention that this trick came from members on our forum, not from me. The savings are monumental. For example, somebody found six nights at the Sheraton Manhattan hotel in Times Square, New York, for £336. Directly booked through the hotel, that would have cost £1,230.

STATE PENSION BOOSTING GUIDE

www.mse.me/statepension

Sometimes we get a little frustrated that the government hasn't built a tool like this. But it hasn't, so we decided to do it.

You only get the full state pension if you've been paying national insurance for enough years. If you haven't paid for enough years, you can 'buy' old years to top it up. Our calculator will show you whether it's worth you buying back these years, and how long you'll have to live after you retire to get your money back. It's useful for a lot of people, from mothers who have taken time off work to people who have lived abroad.

CHEAP IPHONES GUIDE

www.mse.me/iphone

All iPhone packages tend to be pretty horrendous, so the rule is to get yourself in and out of a contract as quickly as possible. This means signing up to a 12-month contract, which means you're paying a bit more – and our guide will show you how much – but you can then jump to a much cheaper tariff and keep your iPhone.

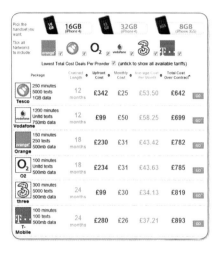

DISCOUNT VOUCHERS

www.mse.me/discountvouchers
www.mse.me/restaurantvouchers
www.mse.me/hotbargains

There are so many discount voucher sites online, and one of the most frustrating things is that many of these sites use clever search-engine optimisation to make you think you're going to get a voucher when it doesn't actually exist. What's more, they report vouchers that don't actually work.

What we promise is that if we put a voucher on our website, we've checked it with the company to make sure it's legitimate. This check is absolutely crucial. And we're not embarrassed to link to other sites if they have a fantastic voucher code.

COUNCIL TAX RECLAIMING GUIDE

www.mse.me/council-tax

We estimate that about 400,000 people are paying too much council tax because they're in the wrong property band. This useful tool lets you check if your home has been placed in the wrong council tax band, so you can see if you're entitled to a rebate. Tens of thousands of people have used this tool to get back thousands of pounds.

FREEBIES FORUM

www.mse.me/freebiesforum

When it comes to money and consumer issues, our forums are just as powerful as Facebook and Twitter, if not more so in some cases. People spot freebies, they share them with others and report the ones that aren't real freebies.

A freebie on this board has to mean absolutely no spend whatsoever – that's no postage and packaging, no having to buy a newspaper – nothing. It has to be completely and genuinely free. It's amazing how many they find, but then if you've got thousands of people searching for them, it's really not that surprising.

OLD STYLE FORUM

www.mse.me/oldstyle

One of the reasons I like the Old Style Forum is that it's not really what I'm about. It was never my idea, and not naturally the sort of thing I'm interested in. You see, Old Style is about thrift.

And I've always said there's a difference between saving money and thrift. My core aim is to cut your bills without cutting back your lifestyle. Let's take toothpaste as an example – I would try to find you a voucher that would knock some money off a tube of toothpaste or explain how to get one for free. The people on the Old Style Forum would say, 'You know, don't buy commercial toothpaste – make it yourself, it's much cheaper'. There are loads of recipe ideas there too, such as 'How to feed your whole family for £15 a week'.

It's all about old-style austerity and the 'make do and mend' attitude – rather than spending money on a mudpack, go and get the mud yourself. It all started from a few discussions on other message boards. One was called: 'Could you live on a World War 2 ration book?' There was also a discussion on how to make your own beauty treatment. I thought they were great, so we gave the idea of thrift its own forum.

DEBT-FREE WANNABE FORUM

www.mse.me/debtfree

If ever you want to cry in a good way, I'd suggest going into the Debt-Free Wannabe Forum, which is a debt-support group. But it's a lot more than holding hands and chanting mantras.

People say that community is dead, but go and have a look at the people in this forum. People are encouraged to come in the first time and give a statement of their situation without revealing their identity. Then everyone else will vulture-like pick over what you're spending money on and tell you what to cut back on. It can be painful for some people, but they call it the lightbulb moment when they know they've got serious debt that they have to deal with.

We have diaries in the forum that people have kept over three or four years, so you can read how they've gone from £80,000 or £90,000 in debt to finally achieving the debt-free day. When you read some of these stories, you'll need a heart of stone not to cry. It's really quite beautiful.

Error 404. Business not found.

Website message not received or understood.
To fix this issue visit: www.wysi.co.uk/error404

Business+ Own a website that converts.

Strengthen your brand.   Convert more visitors.   Communicate online.

Get your Business. Online. with Wysi.co.uk

Find out more:
www.wysi.co.uk/savemoneyonline

Contact the experts now:
t. 0203 292 0536   e. help@wysi.co.uk

business. online.
Websites | CMS | eCommerce | eMarketing | SEO | Reporting | Support

Created with
Adobe ADOBE TECHNOLOGY

wysi.co.uk

BEST FREE SOFTWARE

Essential free
MOBILE APPS

There are thousands of free mobile apps available, but their quality varies greatly. Here's our pick of the best 35 apps for Android, iPhone and the iPad

SAVE MONEY ONLINE

NEW SOFTWARE YOU MUST DOWNLOAD

From addictive puzzle games to complete office suites, the internet is awash with fantastic free programs. But where do you go to find them all? Fortunately, we've done the searching for you

PUZZLE GAMES

ACTIVATE THE THREE ARTEFACTS AND THEN LEAVE
http://bit.ly/activate255
REQUIREMENTS Windows XP/Vista/7, Mac OS X
FILE SIZE 7.3MB

This self-explanatory game starts outside a huge sphere, which is made up of cubes. Fly into this and explore the surroundings, locate the three artefacts hidden somewhere inside, and then return to the exit. It's very easy to get lost, but the atmospheric sounds help guide you in the right direction.

40 STORIES
www.chicostategamestudios.com/40stories
REQUIREMENTS Windows XP/Vista/7
FILE SIZE 305MB

Anita, who works on the 40th floor of an office building, has had enough for the day and wants to go home. Unfortunately the lift isn't working and there are lots of obstacles between her and freedom. The object of the game is to reach the exit on each floor by using terminals to open doors, fax machines to teleport you from one location to another, photocopiers to create helpful clones and so on. You can play through the entire building in sequence, or choose specific levels.

VANESSA SAINT-PIERRE DELACROIX & HER NIGHTMARE
http://bit.ly/van252
REQUIREMENTS Windows XP/Vista/7
FILE SIZE 96.2MB

This puzzle platform game is set on a 3D cube. The aim is to guide Vanessa to the door on each level and exit through it. You can move Miss Saint-Pierre Delacroix left and right, jump and rotate the face of the cube you're currently in. The game gets progressively harder as new elements are introduced. There are keys to find, blocks that have to be placed in markers and people who need to be rescued. Sign up for a free account and you can download additional levels.

QUBE
www.qubegame.co.uk
REQUIREMENTS Windows XP/Vista/7
FILE SIZE 179MB

Qube is a superb 3D puzzle game in a similar vein to the popular Half Life spin-off Valve's Portal. You're equipped with a pair of gloves that let you manipulate the coloured cubes around the levels. The left glove, which is controlled using your left mouse button, extrudes cubes, while the right glove, controlled by the right mouse button, contracts them. As well as red cubes to push in or out, there are blue cubes that can launch you into the air, yellow sets that form stairs and timed blocks. There's no save option, which means you'll have to play through the entire game in one sitting, but it's not too long or overly difficult.

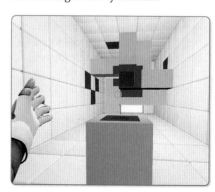

SYSTEM NINJA

www.thewebatom.net
REQUIREMENTS Windows XP/Vista/7
FILE SIZE 653KB

This portable system-cleaning tool is a decent alternative to Piriform's popular CCleaner (www.piriform.com). Rather than targeting files left behind by particular programs, it looks for specific types of junk instead. This includes temporary files, internet cookies and history, thumbnail caches, Windows logs, memory dumps and torrent tags. Select some or all of the items System Ninja has found, click Clear Selected and the software will remove them instantly, freeing up disk space.

System Ninja also offers some additional tools that you can access through tabs along the top of the screen. Startup Manager, for example, displays details of any programs that run alongside Windows, and lets you delete any unnecessary ones. You can manage and remove scheduled tasks from this screen, too.

Process Manager lets you end any currently running processes (proceed with care). If you suspect your PC is infected you can use the MalRun Destroyer tab to identify and kill any processes commonly associated with viruses, spyware and other malware.

Click the More Tools tab to access the Folder Junk Cleaner, which lets you clear out clutter from selected locations, Boot Log Generator and File Analyzr. CCEnhancer, which boosts CCleaner by adding support for another 270 programs, is available here, too.

While System Ninja is a very good free program and can find junk files that other similar tools might miss, it's best used in addition to CCleaner rather than instead of it.

WINMEND AUTO SHUTDOWN

www.winmend.com/auto-shutdown/
REQUIREMENTS Windows XP/Vista/7
FILE SIZE 1.6MB

As the name suggests, this free tool will automatically power down your PC at a scheduled time. Just select a task (Shut Down, Log Off, Sleep or Hibernate) and set a date, time and frequency.

You can also set a countdown and have the computer turn off after that period of time has elapsed.

TOPWINPRIO

http://bit.ly/top255
REQUIREMENTS Windows XP/Vista/7
FILE SIZE 2.1MB

By default, all running applications are given the same priority in Windows. TopWinPrio changes this by automatically diverting more system resources to the program or window that's currently on top – the one you're working in. The difference won't be massive, but you should notice a bit of a boost, particularly on slower systems.

By default the main process priority will be changed to AboveNormal, but you can switch this setting to High or RealTime. You can also lower the priority of all inactive windows.

ENCHANTED KEYFINDER

http://sourceforge.net/projects/ekeyfinder
REQUIREMENTS Windows XP/Vista/7
FILE SIZE 427KB

There's nothing more annoying than being unable to re-install a program you've paid for because you've lost the registration key. This little app scans your Registry and digs out the required details for you. Enchanted Keyfinder can find and display product keys for all versions of Windows and Office and lets you save the information in text format.

SMARTPOWER

http://ignatu.co.uk/SmartPower.aspx
REQUIREMENTS Windows XP/Vista/7
FILE SIZE 556KB

This tiny application gives you greater control over your power-saving settings. You can schedule when your computer should wake up and stay on, and prevent your system hibernating or going to sleep when certain devices are connected, your processor is busy or particular programs are running. SmartPower is very easy to configure and uses minimal system resources.

FILEKILLER

http://filekiller.sourceforge.net
REQUIREMENTS Windows XP/Vista/7
FILE SIZE 22KB

This simple portable application can delete any file on your system for good. Click the Select Files button and browse for the items to remove (unfortunately the program doesn't currently support drag and drop). Choose the number of times you want to overwrite your file(s) and what you want to overwrite them with – this can be random data, blanks or an ASCII character of your choosing. Finally, click the 'Kill Files on Grid' button to remove them permanently.

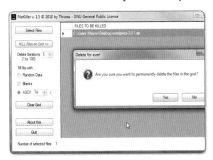

LIBREOFFICE

www.libreoffice.org/download
REQUIREMENTS Windows XP/Vista/7, Mac OS X, Linux
FILE SIZE 138MB

LibreOffice is a spin-off (or rather a fork) of free office suite OpenOffice. org (www.openoffice.org) and is essentially the same product with a new logo. It comprises a word processor, spreadsheet, presentation creator, vector drawing program and a database. These components can be launched individually via the Start menu or accessed through the software's opening splash screen.

If you have OpenOffice.org already there's no reason to upgrade to LibreOffice just yet, especially as the Windows version will overwrite your existing installation. The suite is actively being developed, though, so if you're thinking of trying an alterative to Microsoft Office, this is one to keep an eye on.

LOTUS SYMPHONY

http://symphony.lotus.com
REQUIREMENTS
Windows XP/Vista/7
FILE SIZE 259MB

Symphony is a remixed version of OpenOffice.org (www.openoffice.org), and consists of a word processor, spreadsheet and presentation creator. Each document you create or open appears in a separate tab, so you can switch between different types of office file with ease.

Changes in the latest release include enhanced PDF handling, the ability to embed audio and video files, a new clip art gallery and multi-monitor support for presentations. The new version of the software also adds customisable menu sidebars that provide quick access to text properties and formatting, clip art

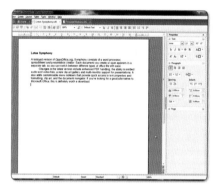

and the document navigator. If you're looking for a good free alternative to Microsoft Office, Symphony is definitely worth downloading.

OPENOFFICE.ORG 3.3

www.openoffice.org
MINIMUM REQUIREMENTS: Windows XP/Vista/7. Mac OS X, Linux
FILE SIZE 151MB

The popular open-source office suite has been updated, and now includes a find toolbar that lets you search inside a document's text, a revamped print interface, support for adding lines and shapes to charts and increased document protection. Slide layout handling has been improved in Impress, and the Calc spreadsheet now supports a whopping one million rows.

SOLACE

http://solacegame.com
REQUIREMENTS Windows XP/Vista/7

FILE SIZE 92.6MB

Solace is a beautiful shoot-'em-up that takes place across the five stages of grief – Denial, Anger, Bargaining, Depression and Acceptance. You can work your way through the stages in order, or play each one separately. The game makes good use of stylish graphics and dynamic audio to convey the changing moods.

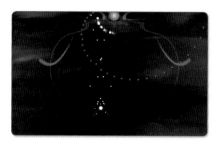

CENFINITY

http://bit.ly/cenfinity251
REQUIREMENTS Windows XP/Vista/7
FILE SIZE 7.5MB

Cenfinity is a shoot-'em-up that takes place in a semi-circle (like half a vinyl record) at the bottom of the screen. Enemies and power-ups come towards you in a clockwise direction and the screen changes colour as you play, which

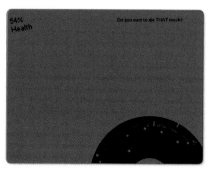

can be quite distracting at times. You can enter the choice of keys you want to use at the start of each game.

INVADERS: CORRUPTION

http://invaders.manuelvandyck.com
REQUIREMENTS Windows XP/Vista/7, Mac OS X
FILE SIZE 10.6MB

Before you can begin playing this game, you'll need to enter a combination of letters and/or numbers to act as a 'core-seed'. This is used to procedurally generate the look of your ship and the incoming invaders, and also determine their attack patterns.

The object is to survive for as long as you can, defeating swarm after swarm of invaders with the aid of power-ups collected along the way.

BEST FREE SOFTWARE

MEDIA PLAYERS

KMPLAYER
http://kmplayer.en.softonic.com
REQUIREMENTS Windows XP/Vista/7
FILE SIZE 6.5MB

This highly customisable player has a minimalist interface and lots of smart touches – the player changes colour when a new song starts, for example. Be sure to decline the PandoraTV search bar during installation, as you can't use it outside the USA.

GOM PLAYER
www.gomlab.com/eng
REQUIREMENTS Windows XP/Vista/7
FILE SIZE 7.2MB

This versatile and powerful media player is packed with features. GOM Player can handle most video formats, including streaming media, Flash video and DVDs. The player also automatically improves the quality of low-resolution videos.

BS PLAYER
www.bsplayer.com
REQUIREMENTS Windows XP/Vista/7
FILE SIZE 13.9MB

BS Player is a well-designed application with a choice of skins. The program will identify and install any missing codecs during installation, which means it should be able to play almost any type of media file.

TASK MANAGERS

TASK LIST GURU
www.dextronet.com/task-list-guru
REQUIREMENTS Windows XP/Vista/7
FILE SIZE 6.1MB

Task List Guru enables you to add and organise tasks, create to-do lists and notes and set reminders. There are 48 coloured icons to apply to your lists, and you can reorder everything simply by dragging and dropping.

TASKUNIFIER
http://taskunifier.sourceforge.net
REQUIREMENTS Windows XP/Vista/7,
Mac OS X, Linux
FILE SIZE 3.6MB

TaskUnifier is a simple Getting Things Done (GTD) manager that lets you divide big tasks into smaller sub-tasks, set goals and organise everything

using folders. You can also synchronise tasks using the online organising tool Toodledo (www.toodledo.com).

WUNDERLIST
www.6wunderkinder.com/wunderlist
REQUIREMENTS Windows XP/Vista/7,
Mac OS X
FILE SIZE 7.69MB

Wunderlist is a simple task-management application that lets you add jobs, set when they're due and then cross them out when complete. You can star tasks,

create lists and filter items by date. You can also search for a task by name – the results appear and are refined as you type. Best of all, if you create an account your tasks will be automatically synced online and across all the computers on which you install Wunderlist.

TASK COACH
www.taskcoach.org
REQUIREMENTS Windows XP/Vista/7,
Mac OS X, Linux
FILE SIZE 10.7MB

Task Coach is a well-designed open-source to-do manager. It lets you create and edit tasks and subtasks in several ways, including dragging and dropping Outlook or Thunderbird emails on to the window. You can add attachments, too, and assign a budget to a task.

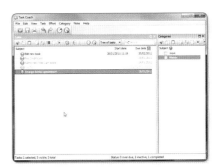

AEROTUNER

http://bit.ly/aerotuner
REQUIREMENTS Windows 7
FILE SIZE 364KB

This tweaking app lets you make some small but useful changes to the Windows Aero interface in Windows 7. The tool lets you pick new main and glow colours, turn off the transparency effect and use sliders to adjust the Colour, After Glow Colour and Blur Balance settings. You can also change how reflective windows appear by tweaking Aero Stripes.

FILERFROG

www.filerfrog.com
REQUIREMENTS Windows XP/Vista/7
FILE SIZE 1.5MB
FilerFrog adds a wealth of useful of commands and tools to the Windows right-click context menu. You can use the program to sort your Desktop icons by type (it will add customisable coloured transparent rectangles behind each group), rename multiple items, split and join files or encrypt and decrypt them, resize photos, convert images to JPG and more. You can add all the functions you're likely to use to a favourites section for quick access. There are 32- and 64-bit versions of the software available.

AEROWEATHER

http://spikex.net
REQUIREMENTS Windows Vista/7 with Aero enabled
FILE SIZE 958KB
This clever little tool automatically changes the colour of Windows Aero based on the current temperature and weather conditions where you are. If you set it to Temperature and it's cold outside, you'll see a deep purple. If it's hot, it will be bright red. You'll mostly see blues, greens and oranges, though. AeroWeather lets you set the temperature range and switch between Fahrenheit and Celsius.

Changing to Conditions will cause Windows to assume a dark grey hue when it's raining, white when snowing and so on. The optional Night Mode dims the Aero colours when the sun sets and brightens them again when it rises the next morning.

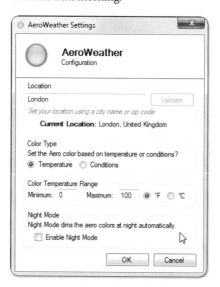

SE-DESKTOPCONSTRUCTOR

http://se-soft.com/en
REQUIREMENTS Windows XP/Vista/7
FILE SIZE 1MB
This simple customisation tool lets you give your Desktop a makeover with an embedded clock, calendar and coloured backdrops for your icons. SE-DesktopConstructor can also change your wallpaper at pre-set intervals. You can adjust the size, position and colour of objects to suit your background, and choose from a decent selection of clock styles, ranging from basic digital displays to fairly outlandish analogue options.

Although the program is very easy to use, getting the size, positioning and transparency of boxes just right does take a little practice as you can't see how they'll look on the Desktop until you apply the changes.

WINDOWS 7 TASKBAR ITEMS PINNER

http://bit.ly/pinner251
REQUIREMENTS Windows 7
FILE SIZE 54.2KB
This tiny portable application lets you pin items to the Windows 7 Taskbar. Run the program in Administrator mode and then tick any of the pre-defined folders to add them. They will appear on the bar immediately.

You can reorder the position of the icons simply by clicking and dragging, and add custom items of your choosing, too. Simply browse for the folder or file you want, select a different icon if necessary and click the Add Item button. The single menu screen shows you all the pinned items and lets you remove any unwanted ones.

PRIVACY TOOLS

SQUARE PRIVACY CLEANER

www.novirusthanks.org
REQUIREMENTS Windows XP/Vista/7
FILE SIZE 697KB

Protect your privacy by removing traces of your activity online and off with this handy cleaning tool. The program can clear temporary and junk files, cookies, browsing history, most recently used (MRU) lists, the clipboard cache, log files and more. Just tick the items you want to remove under each of the tabs and then click the Delete Traces button.

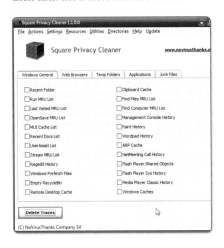

WIPE 2011

http://privacyroot.com
REQUIREMENTS Windows XP/Vista/7
FILE SIZE 4.2MB

Almost everything you do online (and off) gets recorded on your computer. Wipe can prevent hackers and snoopers from spying on your activities by permanently erasing any personal or incriminating data.

The first time you run Wipe, the program will scan your computer to look for supported software. This process can take a while, but it only needs to be done once. When the scan has finished, Wipe will present you with two options – you can delete the tracks and unnecessary files it's found, or access the Advanced cleaning mode and take full control over what to keep and what to remove.

The Advanced mode displays a full list of programs that might contain personal information, and tells you what tracks and junk files can be cleaned. It also shows you how many files and Registry entries are affected and how much disk space will be freed. Scroll down the

list and untick anything you want to keep and then hit the Delete button to remove them. You can also right-click individual entries to view the data that will be cleared.

The Settings button lets you configure the program preferences and set a wipe mode. By default, it just removes files using the standard Windows method, but if you want to prevent files being recovered you can select one of the more secure options. You'll need to register to do this, but it's free and takes a matter of minutes. Wipe also offers a task manager that lets you stop any running programs, as well as a screen-lock function.

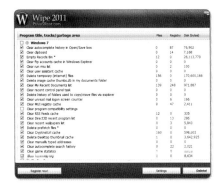

SYSTEM-TOOL SCREENSAVERS

SECURITY ESSENTIALS SCREENSAVER

http://bit.ly/sec253
REQUIREMENTS Windows XP/Vista/7, Microsoft Security Essentials
FILE SIZE 1MB

This screensaver scans your system after a set period of inactivity using Microsoft's excellent Security Essentials anti-malware tool. You'll need to download this separately from www.microsoft.com/security_essentials.

AVAST FREE ANTIVIRUS 5

www.avast.com
REQUIREMENTS Windows XP/Vista/7
FILE SIZE 49.1MB

This free and effective anti-virus program comes with a built-in screensaver mode that can be activated under Settings. You can choose which installed screensaver to display while the program is running.

MYDEFRAG 4

www.mydefrag.com
REQUIREMENTS Windows XP/Vista/7
FILE SIZE 2MB

Although Windows shows files and folders as contiguous items, the reality on your hard disk is rather different. Over time, repeated reading, editing and writing of files inevitably means they become fragmented. This powerful disk-defragmenting tool installs a screensaver that can optimise your hard disk during idle moments. The Windows User Account Control (UAC) feature must be disabled for MyDefrag to work.

DATA-RECOVERY TOOLS

CD RECOVERY TOOLBOX FREE
www.oemailrecovery.com/cd_recovery.html
REQUIREMENTS Windows XP/Vista/7
FILE SIZE 672KB

Even if Windows can't read a damaged disc, this program should still be able to recover at least some data from it. It works with CDs, DVDs and Blu-ray discs. The process can take a while, depending on how damaged the disc is.

MJM FREE PHOTO RECOVERY
http://bit.ly/mjmdatarecovery
REQUIREMENTS Windows XP/Vista/7, Mac OS X
FILE SIZE 3.4MB

This essential little application can help you recover accidentally deleted

EASEUS DATA RECOVERY WIZARD FREE EDITION
www.easeus-deletedrecovery.com
REQUIREMENTS Windows XP/Vista/7
FILE SIZE 3.6MB

This tool lets you retrieve deleted files or data that's been lost through formatting, crashes or partition damage. It offers a choice of modes, but the free version is limited to recovering 1GB of data.

images as well as any pictures that you have stored on corrupt or reformatted memory cards. It provides thumbnail previews of the images, so you can see which photographs the program has found and is able to rescue before you actually recover them.

WORD PROCESSORS

FOCUSWRITER
http://gottcode.org/focuswriter
REQUIREMENTS Windows XP/Vista/7, Mac OS X, Linux
FILE SIZE 5.1MB

This full-screen word processor is designed to remove distractions so you can concentrate on your writing. It's fully customisable and will automatically hide the interface elements until you need them. The word count, character count and other information are updated as you type, and the program autosaves your work.

WRITEMONKEY
http://writemonkey.com/index.php
REQUIREMENTS Windows XP/Vista/7
FILE SIZE 1.8MB

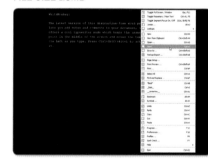

The latest version of this distraction-free word processor lets you add notes and comments to your documents quickly and easily. WriteMonkey also offers a useful typewriter mode that keeps the insertion point in the middle of the screen and moves the text to the left as you type; simply press Ctrl+Shift+Alt+L to activate this feature.

NOTE-TAKING TOOLS

EVERNOTE 4
www.evernote.com
REQUIREMENTS Windows XP/Vista/7
FILE SIZE 38.9MB

This note-taking and web-clipping tool has been redesigned to make it lighter, faster and easier to use. Evernote's clipping and editing processes have both been improved, and the application now supports Windows 7's jump lists and geotagging. You also have greater control over what information to print, and lesser used features now stay hidden out of the way until you need them.

GUMNOTES
www.gumnotes.com
REQUIREMENTS
Windows XP/Vista/7, .NET framework 4
FILE SIZE 6.7MB

Why scribble down notes that you'll lose or spill tea over when you can make digital jottings onscreen? GumNotes lets you annotate anything – from a document to a website or an email – by opening its window in the System Tray and typing your comments. The virtual sticky notes can be private or shared with others, and will appear the next time you view that file or web page.

The notes can also be set to pop up at a certain date/time as reminders. You can hibernate GumNotes for a set duration when it's not required, and use the program in conjunction with Simplenote (http://simplenoteapp.com) to synchronise notes across multiple devices, including Macs, iPhones and Android handsets.

EMAIL PROGRAMS

DREAMMAIL

www.dreammail.eu
REQUIREMENTS Windows XP/Vista/7
FILE SIZE 8.4MB

This Desktop email client offers support for multiple accounts and users. DreamMail boasts an advanced anti-spam filter, RSS manager, address book and a built-in web browser.

Finding messages is very simple thanks to a powerful search tool, and webmail accounts are configured automatically when you enter your username and password.

EMAILTRAY

www.emailtray.com
REQUIREMENTS Windows XP/Vista/7
FILE SIZE 9.8MB

This smart email-notification tool can check multiple webmail and Outlook accounts and alert you when new messages arrive. You can prioritise incoming emails so you'll only be informed about ones you actually care about, and it will even let you send quick replies without needing to open your email client or browser. You can change how the program notifies you, and if you sign up for a free EmailTray account you'll enjoy additional benefits such as improved mail sorting.

RSS TOOLS

FEEDGHOST

www.feedghost.com
REQUIREMENTS Windows XP/Vista/7
FILE SIZE 2.2MB

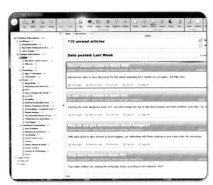

This Desktop RSS reader lets you view and manage web feeds and prioritise your favourites. FeedGhost offers two views – a 'river' of news and a list – and comes with a built-in web browser so you can read full articles without leaving the program. Adding new feeds is very straightforward, and the

TEXT TOOLS

DIFFUSE MERGE TOOL

http://diffuse.sourceforge.net/index.html
REQUIREMENTS Windows XP/Vista/7, Mac OS X, Linux
FILE SIZE 9.5MB

Diffuse Merge Tool is a useful application that lets you compare up to three versions of a text file side by side. The program will highlight any differences and let you merge the ones you want and make any other changes.

The program is designed for comparing code, and offers syntax highlighting for all popular coding languages.

FREEOCR

www.paperfile.net
REQUIREMENTS Windows XP/Vista/7
FILE SIZE 156KB

This optical character recognition (OCR) tool can extract editable text from digital photos, screenshots and scans. It supports a range of image formats, including TIF, JPG, BMP and PDF. You can edit text, correcting any mistakes and removing line breaks, and copy it to your clipboard or open it in your word processor.

software will even suggest new feeds it thinks you might be interested in.

DESKTOP TICKER

www.battware.co.uk/desktopticker.htm
REQUIREMENTS Windows XP/Vista/7
FILE SIZE 326KB

Keep up to date with your favourite web feeds by adding a scrolling RSS/Atom ticker to your Desktop using this tool. You can manage your feeds, dock the ticker to the top or bottom of the screen, change its opacity and speed and set the update frequency. New stories will be shown in red and older ones in black, although you can change the colours to something else if you wish.

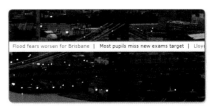

TASK ORGANISER

GEETEEDEE

http://codea-dev.com/gtd
REQUIREMENTS Windows XP/Vista/7
FILE SIZE 4.1MB

This lightweight task organiser will help you manage your workflow and get things done. GeeTeeDee is very easy to use – just click the New button to add a task, give it a name, add some optional details and then set a due date. When you've completed the action, tick the box and it will be crossed out.

You can reorder tasks by clicking and dragging, and remove old ones by dropping them into the Completed or Trash groups. Clicking the Cleanup button will automatically transfer finished jobs into Completed.

Right-clicking the Groups column will let you add new categories, such as Starred, Some Day and To Check.

Essential free
MOBILE APPS

There are thousands of free mobile apps available, but their quality varies greatly. Here's our pick of the best apps for Android, iPhone and the iPad

FIND CHEAP FLIGHTS WITH SKYSCANNER

http://bit.ly/sky262

COMPATIBLE WITH iPhone, iPod Touch, iPad, iOS 3.0+

If you want to find cheap flights, the Skyscanner app can help. It searches over 600 airlines and travel agents and more than 700,000 routes. You can filter the search results by price, airline, stops, time of day, duration and airport, and email flight details to yourself or share with your fellow travellers.

BRING YOUR TEXT MESSAGES TO LIFE

www.chompsms.com

COMPATIBLE WITH Android

ChompSMS is a fun and practical SMS app for Android phones. It lets you conduct lengthy text-message conversations using iPhone-style bubbles, manage unread messages from your home screen and send a quick text even if you're using another app.

ChompSMS also offers signatures, contact pictures, groups of contacts and stacks of customisation features. Messages cost no more than your network's standard rate.

SHARE AND SYNCHRONISE YOUR FILES

www.dropbox.com

COMPATIBLE WITH iPhone, iPad, Android, BlackBerry

Dropbox is so useful we can't remember what life used to be like before this file-sharing service came along. The mobile app lets you back up and download files, sync them across devices and enjoy up to 2GB of storage space for free.

Dropbox works brilliantly on every device, but especially on the iPad, where you can drag and drop photos, videos and web links with ease.

BROWSE WIKIPEDIA LIKE A MAGAZINE

www.cooliris.com/ipad/discover

COMPATIBLE WITH iPad

Free iPad app Discover provides an alternative interface for Wikipedia that transforms the online encyclopedia's functional but dreary interface into a stylish interactive magazine.

Discover makes effective use of all the tapping, dragging and shaking the iPad excels at. For example, you can press a word in an article to view more information about it and shake the device to return to the magazine 'cover'.

PLAN YOUR JOURNEYS IN ADVANCE

http://bit.ly/travel248

COMPATIBLE WITH iPhone, Android

Avoid traffic jams, roadworks and travel chaos with Travel News from Directgov, which uses Department of Transport data for England, Scotland and Wales.

The app is updated regularly and covers public transport as well as major and minor roads, providing up-to-date train departure and arrival times, and displays warnings as pushpins on a Google map. Tap a pin for more information on delays, accidents, restrictions and closed roads.

GET DAILY NEWS FROM THE INDEPENDENT

http://bit.ly/ind248

COMPATIBLE WITH iPhone, iPad

The Independent newspaper offers a superb lightweight iPhone app that downloads around 150 stories (complete with pictures) a day. Downloading takes about a

minute over Wi-Fi or a few minutes on a normal mobile connection, after which you can browse the content offline.

Neatly divided into sections just like a real newspaper, the app lets you specify how long you want to keep articles for, email stories to friends and refresh to read the latest headlines.

TURN YOUR MOBILE PHONE INTO A KEYBOARD

www.remotedroid.net

COMPATIBLE WITH Android

RemoteDroid turns any Android phone into a wireless keyboard and trackpad

that you can use to control your computer. You'll need to download the app for your phone and then a separate server app for your PC, but RemoteDroid is simple to set up, works with your existing wireless network and the results are surprisingly good.

GET IN-DEPTH WEATHER FORECASTS

http://bit.ly/weather248

COMPATIBLE WITH iPhone, iPad

Forget the weedy, uncertain and underpowered weather app that comes with your iPhone – the free AccuWeather. com app is a much better option. It lets you monitor

multiple locations, provides current, hourly and 15-day forecasts and uses clever radar imagery.

It also offers indexes of disruptive weather, alarms for freak conditions and clear, easy-to-understand icons such as lightning to denote a storm.

RECORD TV PROGRAMMES FROM AFAR

http://bit.ly/sky248

COMPATIBLE WITH iPhone, Android

Got a Sky+ or Sky+HD box? Now you don't need to be at home to set up a recording of your favourite TV shows. The Sky+ app comes with a seven-

day channel guide (which works in landscape mode), an 'other airings' option so you can resolve scheduling conflicts and a genre view that helps you sort your sci-fi from your sport.

READ CLASSIC BOOKS ON THE MOVE

http://bit.ly/ibooks248

COMPATIBLE WITH iPhone, iPad

Bookworms will love iBooks, a slick, easy-to-use e-book reader that surpasses similar apps by offering a large selection of free titles by authors that you might actually want to read, such as Charles Dickens, Mark Twain, Herman Melville, AA Milne and Oscar Wilde. There are lots of ways to navigate and customise the app, including browsing your library on a virtual bookshelf.

PLAY CHESS ON THE MOVE

http://bit.ly/chess248

COMPATIBLE WITH iPhone, iPad

Chess Free is a beautifully designed chess game that lets you play against real opponents as well as virtual ones on your iPhone or iPad. There are various degrees

of difficulty, and you can also play against the clock, which is a great way to improve your chess skills.

FIND OUT WHAT'S ON AT THE CINEMA

http://bit.ly/flix248

COMPATIBLE WITH iPhone, iPad

The Movies app from Flixster is good on the iPhone but even better on the iPad. It lets you watch trailers of upcoming feature films and find out when they're showing at your local

cinema. The iPad version uses all that lovely screen space to good effect and proves a great first port of call when you fancy a night at the movies.

TEACH YOURSELF TO PLAY THE PIANO

http://bit.ly/piano248

COMPATIBLE WITH iPhone, iPad

Virtuoso Piano Free is a piano app that looks and sounds like a real piano. It's especially well suited to the iPad because the screen can display two keyboard strips at once.

You use the arrow keys to move the visible keyboard up and down, and add or remove key labels. Click Duette to flip the top keyboard around so someone else can sit opposite you and play along.

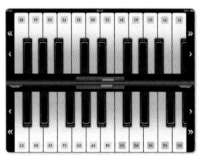

DISCOVER AND SHARE PLACES OF INTEREST

http://gowalla.com

COMPATIBLE WITH iPhone, iPad, Android

Gowalla is a smart location-based social-networking game. It encourages you to find or create 'spots' such as restaurants, bars, theatres and suchlike wherever you go, and then share the details with friends. Gowalla works well with Twitter and Facebook and, although it may cause a bit of head-scratching at first, the idea soon proves oddly addictive.

SEARCH FOR ODEON FILMS

http://bit.ly/odeon262

COMPATIBLE WITH iPhone, iPod Touch, iPad, iOS 3.1+

This app from cinema chain Odeon lets you search for films that are currently showing or coming soon, rate and share them via email and Facebook, view trailers and more. You can use it to find the nearest Odeon cinema, check show times, get directions and securely book tickets. You can also join the Odeon Premiere club and earn points to spend at the cinema.

BUY MUSIC ON THE MOVE

www.7digital.com/mobile

COMPATIBLE WITH Android, BlackBerry

Android and BlackBerry users can buy music on the move from iTunes rival 7digital. The app lets you browse the latest charts, play previews of tracks and listen to songs you've purchased at the best possible quality (up to 320kbps).

GET RECIPES

www.epicurious.com/services/mobile

COMPATIBLE WITH iPhone, Android

You'll never run out of meal ideas with the Epicurious app, which features more than 28,000 recipes and a Shopping List feature that lets you tick off individual ingredients as you buy them.

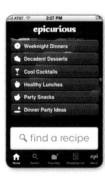

FIND YOUR LOST IPHONE

http://bit.ly/find262

COMPATIBLE WITH iPhone

Designed by Apple itself, this app helps you recover your iPhone 4 should it be lost or stolen by plotting its position on a map. You can remotely delete data, lock the device and have it sound an alarm at full volume.

ADD EFFECTS TO YOUR PHOTOS

http://instagr.am

COMPATIBLE WITH iPhone

This popular iPhone app (which is coming to Android soon) lets you apply 11 fun filter effects to your photos, such as giving them the yellowy appearance of a 70s snap. Instagram also makes it easy to share pictures and view those of your friends.

CHECK IN FOR BA FLIGHTS

http://bit.ly/british262

COMPATIBLE WITH iPhone, Android, BlackBerry

The British Airways app lets you download your boarding pass and use your phone to check in and confirm your seat. This pass is now accepted on all flights from the UK except London City to New York.

USE A VOICE-RECOGNITION APP

www.dragonmobileapps.com

COMPATIBLE WITH iPhone

Dragon Dictation is a voice-recognition app that lets you speak text content for emails, social-networking updates and blog posts. It instantly translates your words and even lets you switch between different languages.

IDENTIFY NAMES OF SONGS

www.shazam.com

COMPATIBLE WITH iPhone, Android, BlackBerry, Windows, Symbian

If you want to know the name of a song being played on TV, in a shop or a pub, simply hold your phone up to the music source and Shazam will identify the mystery tune. The free version lets you 'tag' up to five tracks per month.

CHECK FOR DAYS OUT VIA THE NATIONAL TRUST

http://bit.ly/national262

COMPATIBLE WITH iPhone, Android

If you fancy a day out in the country, the National Trust app will give you ideas for places to go. It features more than 400 entries, ranging from stately homes to stunning scenery, and provides details of opening times, prices and directions.

MONITOR YOUR EXERCISE

http://bit.ly/cardio262

COMPATIBLE WITH Android

This fitness app has everything you need to track your exercise activity. CardioTrainer lets you trace your running route via GPS, count the number of steps you've walked, tot up the calories you've consumed, monitor your heart rate and much more.

PROTECT AGAINST MALWARE

www.mylookout.com

COMPATIBLE WITH Android, BlackBerry, Windows

With mobile malware on the rise, Lookout protects your phone for free. As well as detecting and removing viruses, it lets you back up data over the air.

EASILY UNINSTALL APPS

http://bit.ly/uninstaller262

COMPATIBLE WITH Android

Apps aren't as easy to remove from Android devices as they are on the iPhone, which has a dedicated Delete option. Uninstaller remedies this by letting you get rid of apps you don't want with a single click. App Cleaner (http://bit.ly/appcleaner262) is also good.

EXPERIENCE A NEW REALITY

www.layar.com

COMPATIBLE WITH iPhone, Android

This augmented-reality app uses your phone's GPS sensor to establish your location, turns on your camera and applies 'layers' of information, such as nearby cashpoints, restaurants and stations. Wikitude (www.wikitude.org), available for Android, iPhone and Symbian, is also worth a look.

BEST FREE SOFTWARE

Get your website online in minutes
and make @ name for yourself!

We offer a range of solutions that suit all needs, from **personalised email** with spam and virus protection to **business web hosting** including **FREE .uk domain** and **eshop facility**.

With over 10 years' experience we're the web host you can trust. With **free setup** and **24/7 phone** and **online support** we're here whenever you need us, day or night.

HALF PRICE ON SELECTED PACKAGES*

HOSTING NOW UP TO 50% OFF FOR 3 MONTHS*

Email hosting you@yourname.com

It's easy to create a personalised email address using your own domain. Plus get 50% off for 3 months with our exchange packages.

MAIL PLUS
£14.99pa (£17.99 inc VAT)
Annual payment applies

Professional email using your own domain
- ✔ 5 flexible mailboxes (50MB each)
- ✔ 2 Virus & spam protected mailboxes
- ✔ Fasthosts Webmail
- ✔ POP3 & IMAP access

EXCHANGE – HALF PRICE
£4.99pm (£5.99 inc VAT)
Normal price £11.99 inc VAT

Email hosting designed for any business
- ✔ 5 flexible mailboxes (50MB each)
- ✔ 1 Exchange mailbox (2GB each)
- ✔ Fasthosts Webmail
- ✔ Individual mailbox control panel
- ✔ Mobile access for real-time updates

ALL PACKAGES INCLUDE:
- ✔ Autoresponders
- ✔ Individual mailbox control panels
- ✔ Secure UK data centre
- ✔ Catch-all email

Check online for details on easy mobile access

Web hosting

Create a professional looking website quickly and easily with our free and simple to use website builder. Plus get up to 50% off for 3 months.

PERSONAL STANDARD – 10% OFF
£4.49pm (£5.39 inc VAT)
Normal price £5.99 inc VAT

- ✔ 5GB web space
- ✔ Unlimited bandwidth†
- ✔ Choice of Windows or Linux (no extra cost)
- ✔ Virus & spam protected email
- ✔ FREE website builder
- ✔ FREE instant setup

BUSINESS STANDARD – 30% OFF
£6.29pm (£7.55 inc VAT)
Normal price £10.79 inc VAT

- ✔ 25GB web space
- ✔ Unlimited bandwidth†
- ✔ Choice of Windows or Linux (no extra cost)
- ✔ FREE website builder
- ✔ FREE instant setup
- ✔ FREE .uk domain (worth £5.90)
- ✔ FREE £105 advertising vouchers
- ✔ 5 MySQL databases
- ✔ ASP.NET 3.5 with AJAX extensions
- ✔ OneClick Installer (Linux only)

goMobi now available
*our **new** mobile website builder***

We have a wide range of domains available **from £2.95pa. Secure yours today!**

Buy now at
fasthosts.co.uk/hosting
0844 583 0776

Microsoft GOLD CERTIFIED Partner

Proud sponsor of
The Great Exhibition 2012

World Class Web Hosting

FIND HIDDEN BARGAINS

p36

Find the web's
CHEAPEST PRICES

Price-comparison sites are a great way to find bargains online, but which will save you the most money? We test seven of the most popular services

Foundem
★★★★★
www.foundem.co.uk

EASE OF USE ★★★★★   FEATURES ★★★★☆   RANGE ★★★★☆   SAVING POTENTIAL ★★★★★

WHAT WE LIKE

Foundem gets most of the fundamentals of a price-comparison search spot on: the all-important search bar sits at the top, with a selection of clickable product categories below.

Perform a search and the site automatically orders the results, with the cheapest at the top. Of course, the cheapest isn't necessarily the best or most appropriate deal, but it's undoubtedly the best starting point for most users of price-comparison sites.

Digging a bit deeper, an interesting part of Foundem is the Best Price History chart that's displayed when you drill down to view particular items. This shows you, for example, that the price of coffee machines tends to dip in summer, so if you're in the market for a fancy cappuccino-maker, it may be best to avoid buying one during the colder months.

Foundem covers an impressive range of products, although it lacks the breadth of our Bronze-award winner PriceRunner, which is as

happy comparing the prices of gas and electricity as the latest must-have gadgets. The most impressive thing about Foundem, though, is the simple fact that in our tests it found the best deals with the minimum of fuss.

HOW IT CAN BE IMPROVED

Foundem occasionally presented results that were entirely incongruous with our search terms. When hunting

for a hiking jacket, for example, we don't expect to be offered prices for men's fragrances and children's toys.

OUR VERDICT

Foundem proved a good bet for finding the best prices on even obscure items. The site looks sparse compared to some of the price-comparison sites reviewed here, but we consider this an advantage.

GOLD

Kelkoo

★★★★☆

www.kelkoo.co.uk

EASE OF USE ★★★★★ FEATURES ★★★★☆ RANGE ★★★★☆
SAVING POTENTIAL ★★★★★

WHAT WE LIKE

Kelkoo provides several ways to search, including by keyword, brand and store. The shopping categories cover everything from barbecues to TVs, and although it's annoying that search results are sorted by popularity by default, they're easy to reorder by price.

Kelkoo has been part of the Yahoo stable of companies since 2004, with all the strategic alliances that entails. As such, the 'powered by Kelkoo' message pops up on numerous rival price-comparison services. But there are some things Kelkoo is keeping to itself, such as the Kelkoo toolbar and cashback system. Use a Kelkoo link to buy something from Kodak Gallery, for example, and you'll earn 9 per cent back on your purchase. The cashback percentage ranges from 1.2 to 15 per cent, and Kelkoo sends you a cheque when your account balance hits £12.

HOW IT CAN BE IMPROVED

Although the site alerts you to wrong or out-of-date information, the option to continue to the retailer remains.

OUR VERDICT

Kelkoo is a popular site for good reasons – it's easy to use, effective at finding bargains and offers a great cashback scheme.

PriceRunner

★★★★☆

www.pricerunner.co.uk

EASE OF USE ★★★★★ FEATURES ★★★★☆ RANGE ★★★★★
SAVING POTENTIAL ★★★★☆

WHAT WE LIKE

PriceRunner may look much like any other price-comparison site – although it has more products than most – but it works a bit harder than other sites at presenting relevant advice and current deals. Perform a search and PriceRunner shows you current offers and voucher codes for the product, as well as prices.

This idea is extended to buying advice, with mixed results: when searching for a Russell Hobbs kettle, for example, we were offered guidance on shopping for mobile phones.

Elsewhere, the product reviews and forums seem handy, but the nature of price-comparison sites means most contributors don't hang around for long.

HOW IT CAN BE IMPROVED

Seeing related offers and voucher codes alongside search results is useful, but the information provided isn't always accurate. Stronger links between reviews and the forum would make it easier to check the credentials of reviewers.

OUR VERDICT

PriceRunner's price results were on a par with Kelkoo's. However, the added incentive of Kelkoo's cashback system means PriceRunner has to settle for the Bronze award.

BEST OF THE REST

PriceGrabber.co.uk

www.pricegrabber.co.uk
PriceGrabber.co.uk's stand-out feature is SHOPgreen, a service that only compares goods that are supposedly less damaging to the environment. We were also impressed by the Free Delivery section, where you can view the cheapest deals on popular products without any hidden delivery charges.

Shopping.com

http://uk.shopping.com
Shopping.com presents results in a confusing manner, placing 'sponsored' matches at the top of results list and not making it clear which are the cheapest deals. What's more, it didn't find any particularly good deals.

PriceTerrier.com

http://shop.priceterrier.com
PriceTerrier.com is basically Kelkoo with a different skin. Owner ITV has altered the name, added an image of a sniffing mutt and that's about it. So, while it boasts most of the same pros and cons as Kelkoo and can find bargains across a wide range of categories, you might as well stick with Kelkoo.

Twenga

www.twenga.co.uk
Twenga claims to be the UK's most comprehensive shopping-search engine, but its layout is a mish-mash of links, tabs and frames that make your eyes work too hard. This continues on the results page, where listings are confusingly organised under meaningless headings such as 'Top' and 'Best'.

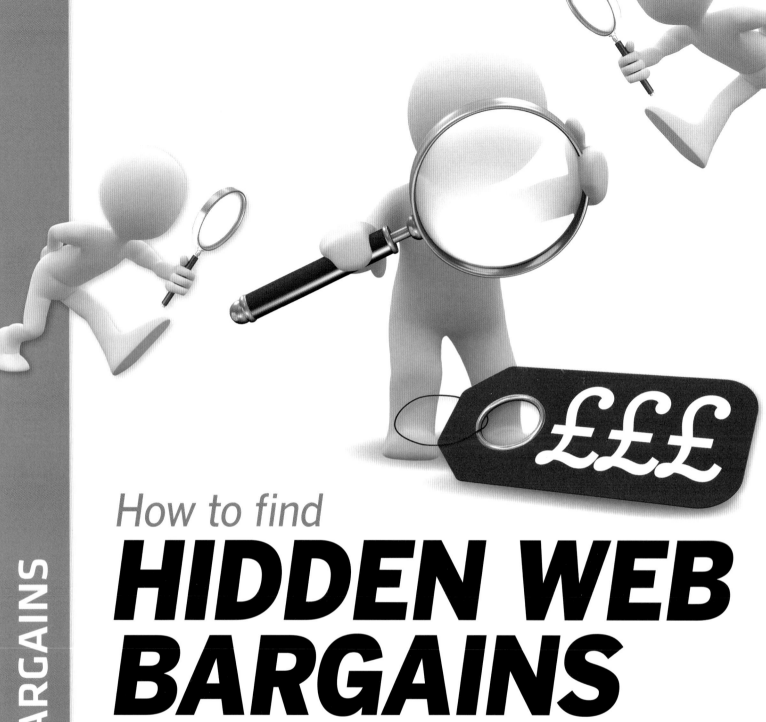

How to find
HIDDEN WEB BARGAINS

Price-comparison sites can help you find some great online bargains, but you can often uncover cheaper deals if you do the hunting yourself. Over the next few pages, we explain how

One of the best things about shopping on the web is that you can check out an enormous variety of products without having to slog up and down the high street. Indeed, thanks to price-comparison websites, you can find online bargains with barely any effort. These sites provide a fast and simple way to compare prices, but do they always take you straight to the cheapest deals?

The truth is that while price-comparison services are undeniably useful, you'll often find better online bargains away from these aggregators. Although price-comparison sites can quickly search through a database of retailers, they don't search every single outlet on the web. Indeed, some services actively encourage you to click on links served up by affiliate sites they have deals with, even when these aren't the cheapest options.

Provided you know where to look, you can usually beat the price-comparison sites at their own game. Over the next few pages, we provide a 10-step guide to uncovering the best hidden web bargains to help cut the cost of your shopping online.

STEP 1

START WITH THE PRICE-COMPARISON SITES

It might sound like we're contradicting ourselves right off the bat, but the purpose of this feature is to beat price-comparison sites, not ignore them completely. Our aim is to help you find the best possible deals online, and often price-comparison sites do just that.

Moreover, these services remove an awful lot of the calculations involved in assessing the overall cost – totting up postage and packing fees and including any additional charges. So, if you're shopping for a particular item, we'd suggest starting with a visit to at least one price-comparison service, even if it's just for research purposes.

In this feature, we've used Foundem (www.foundem.co.uk), PriceRunner (www.pricerunner.co.uk) and Kelkoo (www.kelkoo.co.uk) – the three winners in our test on pages 28-29 – as starting points: in all cases we've beaten both their results – by hundreds of pounds,

in a few instances – but sometimes there's little or no advantage in going it alone. For example, both PriceRunner and Kelkoo served up very similar deals for an Acer Aspire laptop, with £358.80 and £360.48 respectively. Despite our best efforts, we could better the lowest of these prices by only a few pence. Conversely, when searching for a Belkin router, Kelkoo told us the best deal was £46.34 from Amazon (www.amazon.co.uk). We found the same router listed for £11 less elsewhere in the store, which Kelkoo evidently missed.

PriceRunner also has a free iPhone app (http://bit.ly/price254) that lets you compare prices on the move and an excellent blog called The Insider (http://theinsider.pricerunner.co.uk), which features helpful buying guides and reviews. Kelkoo, meanwhile, provides a cashback toolbar (http://cashback.kelkoo.co.uk), which highlights money-back deals as you browse the web.

In short, don't completely abandon your price-comparison bookmarks; just bear in mind that they represent only one part of your cost-cutting armoury.

STEP 2

CHECK OUT CLEARANCE AUCTIONS

While the sales departments of high-street and online stores are busy shipping out shiny new goods, their returns divisions are dealing with customers' unwanted items. Some of these products may be faulty, while others have suffered cosmetic damage in transit or have been returned under the Distance Selling Regulations Act (http://bit.ly/distance254) but can't be resold as new because the original packaging is no longer intact.

In these situations, the goods become clearance items. Many well-known and respected retailers now run secondary – but separate – operations to offload these items at cut prices.

One of the best of these sites is Clearance Comet (www.clearance-comet.co.uk), where the high-street electrical store Comet (www.comet.co.uk) auctions off all manner of scuffed, refurbished and otherwise surplus products. When we visited the site, we found an Altec Lansing IM600 iPod speaker dock selling

for £68.95 including delivery. It was described as slightly scratched, but the Clearance Comet price was 30 per cent cheaper than anywhere else we found that sold the product, even with the help of price-comparison sites. All products come with a six-month warranty.

Some companies have decided that it's not worth setting up a dedicated clearance website and have instead turned to eBay (www.ebay.co.uk) to host their discount stores. Argos, for example, has an eBay outlet store (http://stores.ebay.co.uk/Argos-Outlet) that's packed with refurbished products. These clearance auctions are always worth checking if you're looking for a bargain, especially on hardware and other consumer electronics.

STEP 3

BROWSE EBAY FOR FIXED-PRICE BARGAINS

These days, eBay sells as many brand-new products as it does second-hand items, many at knockdown prices. For this reason, it sometimes pays to ignore auction lots and focus purely on the fixed-price Buy It Now listings.

When you're searching for an item, click the New box under Condition in the left-hand options menu to narrow down the listings to new goods at fixed prices. This strategy will make it much easier to compare prices found on eBay with those on other official outlets.

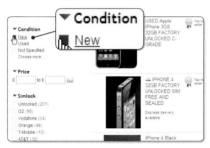

There's an important caveat: don't forget to factor in postage and packaging charges. Many crafty sellers list items on eBay at very low headline prices and make up the difference with inflated postage costs. To be fair to eBay, it has taken strides to crack down on this practice, most recently by introducing maximum postage and packaging for a range of product categories. Even so, sellers can still charge up to £8 P&P, even on small items, so watch out.

That's not the only pricing trickery at play on eBay. Some of the most

attractive headline prices originate from sellers outside the UK. This isn't a great concern in itself – you're just as likely to deal with honest traders based in China as get scammed by someone in Chester – but goods shipped from overseas may attract import taxes when they arrive in the UK. The rules and laws governing this area are confusing and complex – not least because even the HMRC (www.hmrc.gov.uk) isn't always consistent in its interpretations – but if you're buying expensive goods from overseas sellers, it's wise to check the specific regulations (read them at http://bit.ly/pricecomp1254).

As always with eBay, check the seller's feedback before you buy anything and keep an eye out for suspicious activity. If feedback has been gained solely for buying rather than selling items, treat the seller as if they have no feedback at all. Also, watch out for fake items,

especially designer names, and be wary if the photo accompanying a listing is a generic image from a company website rather than a photo taken by the seller of the particular item being sold.

If you can't find a decent bargain on eBay, try rival auction site eBid (http://uk.ebid.net). When we visited, there were more than 27,000 products being sold in the Computing category alone. The site also offers an invaluable 'calculate' function that works out the true cost of buying items from abroad.

STEP 4

SEARCH FOR VOUCHER CODES

There are now plenty of voucher-code-sharing sites, designed to keep you informed of the very latest and best offers online. Both MyVoucherCodes.co.uk (www.myvouchercodes.uk) and VoucherCodes.co.uk (www.vouchercodes.co.uk) feature a massive variety of discounts from big-name retailers as well as some lesser-known shops.

Unfortunately, price-comparison websites aren't terribly good at incorporating discount codes into their listings, which prevents you from landing some great bargains. That's not

to say that they ignore discount vouchers altogether – PriceRunner and Kelkoo have dedicated voucher sections, and smaller sites such as Billy Bargain (www.billybargain.co.uk) also carry codes – but

the potential for additional price cuts from vouchers isn't usually factored into your search results.

A better idea is to visit the excellent HotUKDeals (www.hotukdeals.com), which found us a £5-off voucher code for the best-selling game Call of Duty: Black Ops. The best price found by comparison sites for the Xbox version was £39.90. With our discount voucher, however, we could have bought it for £34.99 from Tesco Entertainment (www.tescoentertainment.com).

It's also worth installing the MyVoucherCodes.co.uk toolbar

(http://myvouchercodes.ourtoolbar.com) for Internet Explorer, Firefox, Chrome and Safari. This alerts you to discounts as you browse the web and delivers news of the latest deals directly to your Desktop.

If you're planning to purchase a specific item or shop at a particular online store, it's always worth checking if any live voucher codes are available that could cut your costs.

STEP 5

SIGN UP FOR MONEY-SAVING EMAILS

Our suggestions so far have all required a degree of active participation on your part, but you could just sit back and wait for the latest deals come straight to you: simply sign up for one of the countless money-saving newsletters now available.

The best is from MoneySavingExpert.com (www.moneysavingexpert.com – see pages 6-10). Sign up for the Free MoneySaving Email (www.moneysavingexpert.com/news) and every week you'll receive a summary of the best and most interesting deals from the past few days. Many of these are exclusive to MoneySavingExpert.com or have a very short shelf life, so it's a great way to stay informed about offers without having to hunt around.

The CamelCamelCamel (http://uk.camelcamelcamel.com) website is another useful shopping tool that provides a free service offering alerts and historical price charts for all products listed on Amazon (www.amazon.co.uk). When the cost of an item you want drops to a certain level or below, CamelCamelCamel will email you an alert so you can snap it up for a bargain price.

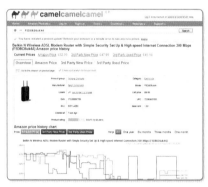

STEP 6

INSTALL THE INVISIBLEHAND ADD-ON

Another way to avoid the effort of actively tracking down bargains is to install a browser add-on to do the job for you. The excellent InvisibleHand (www.getinvisiblehand.com) – available for IE, Firefox, Chrome and Safari – will pop up to alert you whenever it detects that a product you're viewing in an online store can be bought cheaper elsewhere.

We installed the add-on in our Firefox browser and then went shopping for a variety of goods at different online stores. When looking at computer kit on Amazon, InvisibleHand regularly stepped in to alert us to lower prices. One warning slashed 8 per cent – a total of £56.65 – off the price of a 13.3in Sony Vaio notebook if we bought it from Laptops Direct (www.laptopsdirect.co.uk) rather than Amazon.

The only flaw with InvisibleHand – one that the developers acknowledge and are working to fix – is that the tool doesn't take account of postage and packing charges (though it does list them alongside links to the online store). This means that some of the cheaper deals it flags up could actually end up costing you more once you factor in extra charges. Still, InvisibleHand is free and it's a brilliant tool for bargain-hunters.

SAVE MONEY ON THE MOVE

UPC (6, 12 digits)
Scans: EAN (8, 13 digits)
QR Code

Align barcode edges with arrows.

Model No. E3000-UK

Most of the ideas suggested here can be just as easily performed on mobile devices as on a desktop computer. However, there are a number of handy smartphone apps available that can save you even more money when you're out and about.

Having a barcode-scanning application installed on your handset could save you a packet when you're shopping in the high street. Our favourite is RedLaser (www.redlaser. com), which is owned by eBay and is available for the iPhone and Android handsets. You simply point your phone at a product's barcode, and within seconds RedLaser will return results from eBay's Shopping.com (http://uk.shopping.com) price-comparison service to tell you if you can buy the item for less online.

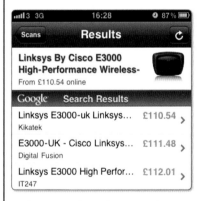

...l 3 3G	16:28	87%
Scans	**Results**	

Linksys By Cisco E3000 High-Performance Wireless-
From £110.54 online

Google   Search Results

Linksys E3000-uk Linksys... Kikatek	£110.54 >
E3000-UK - Cisco Linksys... Digital Fusion	£111.48 >
Linksys E3000 High Perfor... IT247	£112.01 >

ShopSavvy (www.biggu.com) is a similar app available for both iPhone and Android handsets (and on the way for BlackBerry and Windows Phone 7), although it's not quite as easy to use as RedLaser. The app uses the PriceGrabber (www. pricegrabber.co.uk) comparison service to compare prices.

CONSIDER A SWAP

Now for a little lateral thinking: do you need to bother finding the lowest prices for products at all? Instead, you could look around your home for things you no longer need, because it's possible to exchange almost anything using online swapping services.

GaBoom (www.gaboom.co.uk), for example, is a game-swapping website that featured in the most recent series of *Dragons' Den*. The student founder didn't receive investment, but she ploughed on regardless and has built a great service. Remember that 'Call of Duty: Black Ops' bargain we found earlier? Well, £34.99 may be a good price for a new title, but if you have games to swap you could actually get it for free using GaBoom's trust-based forum exchange. If you'd prefer to have buyer protection, the site's Secure Swap service costs £4.40 (the other party also has to pay £4.40, but that's not your concern). See GaBoom's explanation page at www.gaboom.co.uk/how-it-works for full details of each option.

While GaBoom deals just with games, other online swapping sites

have a broader range of goods up for exchange. At Swapz.co.uk (www. swapz.co.uk), for example, you can find people wanting to swap anything from postage stamps to luxury cars. However, it must be pointed out that this is a time-consuming and labour-intensive way of bargain-hunting: it can take days for potential swappers to hammer out a deal, and you need to take great care over the details when making a trade. But if you want to get your hands on cheap hardware while clearing out some cupboard space, then Swapz.co.uk is well worth a try.

You'll also find some great stuff at SwapShop.co.uk (www.swapshop.co.uk), which lets you create a wish-list of items that you're after.

BAG A SECOND-HAND BARGAIN

If the product you want to buy doesn't need to be immaculate, consider delving into the second-hand market and sifting through the classified sections of Craigslist (www.craigslist.com) and Gumtree (www.gumtree.com).

Both sites are home to hundreds of thousands of ads for second-hand goods, organised by product category and region, so it's easy to find someone local selling the item you want. Gumtree even offers email alerts (http://alerts. gumtree.com) to notify you when something you want becomes available.

However, the obvious caveats apply when dealing with pre-owned products. For starters, don't pay a penny until you have the goods in your hands and, even

then, check the items very carefully before handing over your cash to make sure they're not damaged and are exactly as they were described by the seller.

If you want to buy second-hand goods – either to save money or to help the environmental – but are worried about being ripped off, why not give recycling sites a go? All the second-hand goods advertised on Freecycle (www.freecycle.org) and Freegle (www.ilovefreegle.org) are completely free. The sites rely on generous types whose motive is not to make a profit but simply wish to reduce the amount of stuff that goes to landfill.

On the day we checked our local Freecycle group, there was an offer to collect a 'good as new' 17in LCD monitor. However, you've got to be alert and act fast: most items are bagged in minutes. The period immediately after Christmas is a good time to visit, when people offload unwanted gifts.

STEP 9

COMPARE THE PRICE-COMPARERS

Because price-comparison sites search a set number of retailers, their results are inevitably limited to the products those stores have in stock. Fortunately, you can get around this by using MegaShopBot.com (www.megashopbot.com). The idea behind this free tool from MoneySavingExpert.com is that you send your bargain-hunting requests to several price-comparison services at once to find the cheapest deals without needing to visit individual sites.

MegaShopBot.com's founding principle serves as a reminder of the risk of relying on any single price-comparison site: specifically, that the discounts they dish up may depend on their own business alliances, rather than your best interests.

MegaShopBot.com can search up to a dozen price-comparison sites at the same time, including big names such as 123PriceCheck (www.123pricecheck.co.uk), Twenga (www.twenga.co.uk) and

Foundem (www.foundem.co.uk). We used the tool to find the best online deal for the *Toy Story 3* DVD. Had we gone straight to Kelkoo, we would have paid £15.85 for the movie while, shockingly, PriceRunner couldn't find it at all. But, thanks to MegaShotBot.com, we picked up a copy for just £9.97 from Find-DVD.co.uk (www.find-dvd.co.uk) – a fantastic saving of 59 per cent.

STEP 10

SEARCH FOR CASHBACK DEALS

To earn money as you shop at a wide variety of retailers, you'll find cashback deals galore at Top CashBack (www.topcashback.co.uk) and Quidco (www.quidco.com).

When we visited, these included a 10.1 per cent cashback on Alienware PCs and laptops from Dell (www.topcashback.co.uk/dell) and five per cent cashback on all online orders – excluding entertainment products – from Best Buy (www.quidco.com/best-buy). Top CashBack also has a toolbar (http://topcashback.ourtoolbar.com) that lets you search for deals as you shop.

Get the best
DISCOUNTS ONLINE

There's no shortage of voucher-code websites, but which ones offer the best deals? We rate the top money-saving sites to find the best places to bag a bargain

MyVoucherCodes.co.uk

★★★★★

www.myvouchercodes.co.uk

EASE OF USE ★★★★★   FEATURES ★★★★☆   DISCOUNTS ★★★★★   COMMUNITY ★★★★★

WHAT WE LIKE

MyVoucherCodes.co.uk has a reputation for having a clean presentation, being very easy to use and for offering an incredible number of discounts. But is it still the king of online savings? The answer is a resounding 'yes'.

The site now features discounts from more than 8,500 retailers and has made some interesting improvements in the past year or so. A number of exclusive and good-quality deals have been added – for example, you can get 10 per cent off a room at Hotels.com (www.hotels.com) and a 20 per cent discount at Harveys (www. harveysfurniture.co.uk) – most of which we didn't find on rival sites.

Other useful features include the Free Delivery section, which collects offers that won't charge you anything for postage and packing, and a Top 50 list of the most popular discounts. We also like the option to browse live voucher codes by different categories so you can see the latest savings as they become available.

One particularly intriguing feature is called Local. This section provides details of small businesses that are offering region-specific discounts – a welcome bonus on an already packed site.

The MyVoucherCodes. co.uk blog continues to be friendly and informative, drawing attention to noteworthy savings, and there's a toolbar for IE, Firefox and Safari that alerts you to codes as you browse.

HOW IT CAN BE IMPROVED

We wish the site would delete codes as soon as they expire so that you don't get excited about an old offer. Also, there were no printable food or clothing vouchers when we looked.

OUR VERDICT

MyVoucherCodes.co.uk has gone from strength to strength. It's a great site that provides a huge range of discounts for all kinds of products and services.

VoucherCodes.co.uk

★★★★☆

www.vouchercodes.co.uk

SILVER

EASE OF USE ★★★★★ **FEATURES** ★★★★☆ **DISCOUNTS** ★★★★★ **COMMUNITY** ★★☆☆☆

WHAT WE LIKE

VoucherCodes.co.uk's strongest point is its printable vouchers section, which features a huge variety of offers for restaurants, days out, high-street shops, gyms and more, with the latest offers included in a weekly newsletter. There are lots of online discounts, too, including many that are exclusive to VoucherCodes.co.uk.

Previously, VoucherCodes.co.uk didn't let you copy and paste codes into the relevant boxes on websites, and there were no RSS feeds. Both of these issues have been resolved and you can now get feeds for deals from individual stores as well as for new, featured and expiring discounts. We also like the online magazine, Most Wanted, which features all the latest shopping news.

HOW IT CAN BE IMPROVED

VoucherCodes.co.uk could do with more reviews of shops and would benefit from improved social-networking elements, other than merely providing links to Facebook and Twitter.

OUR VERDICT

VoucherCodes.co.uk is constantly improving. The site's exclusive deals and printable vouchers help it stand out from the crowd, and the smart presentation makes it a joy to use.

ShoppingVouchers.co.uk

★★★★☆

www.shoppingvouchers.co.uk

BRONZE

EASE OF USE ★★★★★ **FEATURES** ★★★★☆ **DISCOUNTS** ★★★★★ **COMMUNITY** ★★☆☆☆

WHAT WE LIKE

ShoppingVouchers.co.uk's attractive interface displays a selection of featured stores and exclusive offers, such as 10 per cent discounts at Expedia (www.expedia.co.uk) and Tesco (www.tesco.com).

Scroll down and you'll find specific products you can buy using the codes on offer, which is great if you're looking for inspiration. Indeed, the site seems to thrive on helpful shopping suggestions – the Twitter feed announces deals of the day and there's a blog that highlights particularly interesting bargains. You're encouraged to share discounts with others – pages can be emailed, tweeted or posted on Facebook – and, if you sign up for a free account, the site will send you offer alerts for your favourite stores. You can cut and paste voucher codes, and offers can be rated and commented on.

HOW IT CAN BE IMPROVED

The printable vouchers section could be better organised, and we'd also like to see the lesser-known stores given prominence among the big names.

OUR VERDICT

ShoppingVouchers.co.uk keeps things simple but has lots of great bargains. Hopefully, the community will build as more people sign up.

BEST OF THE REST

DiscountVouchers.co.uk

www.discountvouchers.co.uk

We were amazed by some of the eye-catching offers at DiscountVouchers.co.uk, such as £15 off flexible-rate bookings at Travelodge and 10 per cent off at Ann Summers. It currently lacks the sharing and community tools of the better-known sites, however.

VoucherKing.co.uk

www.voucherking.co.uk

VoucherKing.co.uk handily places a host of printable vouchers on the homepage. We like the way retailers can be recommended with a star rating and that you can easily view vouchers that have just been added. There are some strange quirks – it suggested Ford as a similar store to Expedia – but it's still a good site.

Edeals

www.edeals.com/uk

Edeals doesn't have any printable vouchers (at least, not yet – the US version has them so we assume they're coming soon), but it does have a handy iPhone app. Some big names, including Apple and Argos, are mixed in with smaller retailers. It still seems to be finding its feet, but it looks promising.

Codes.co.uk

www.codes.co.uk

Codes.co.uk has plenty of deals for niche retailers, which is good if you don't always want to shop at big-name stores. The design is great and you can comment on discounts and share them with friends. It has a blog and Twitter feed and is particularly good for travel savings.

BOOST YOUR PC

p40

p50

p52

BOOST YOUR PC

Group test
DNS SERVERS

Can changing your DNS server boost the speed and security of your internet connection? We test three free packages to find out

OpenDNS
★★★★★
www.opendns.com

BOOST YOUR PC

p54

SAVE MONEY ONLINE

A faster PC
FOR FREE

Regular PC maintenance can prevent the majority of computer woes. Here are 30 free and easy ways to keep your system safe and healthy

Computers have become such an integral part of our lives that we often take them for granted. It can be easy to forget just how complicated they actually are – until they start going wrong.

PCs can fail, freeze, crash and stall in all sorts of infuriating and bewildering ways. Identifying the source of your computer's woes isn't always straightforward, however, and solving the problem often involves a fair degree of trial

and error. In the worst cases you may even have to resort to technical support, which can cost a lot of money.

If you want to avoid unnecessary headaches with Windows, it's important to act now. A spot of regular maintenance is all that's required to keep your PC running in tip-top condition for the next few years. Over the next few pages, we explain 30 free and easy ways to get your PC fighting fit using the latest software, tools and techniques.

OPTIMISE YOUR COMPUTER

STOP PROGRAMS RUNNING ON STARTUP

So many programs set themselves to start alongside Windows that it can take an age for the operating system to load. WhatInStartup (http://bit.ly/what255) is a tiny 50KB tool that lets you delete, modify and disable programs that run when Windows starts up. The program provides a wealth of information on each item in the startup list, including its type (whether it's in the Registry or the startup folder), product name, location, process path and more.

SPEED UP YOUR STARTUP WITH SOLUTO

Soluto (www.soluto.com), which was launched in 2010 and is currently still in beta, monitors the boot process and tells you exactly how long it takes to complete. This is usually a lot longer than you'd think, as items continue to load in the background even after the Desktop has appeared.

When it's finished analysing your startup, Soluto presents a comprehensive list of auto-running applications that are safe to remove or delay. Every time you kill an item, the boot time will change so you can see how many seconds you've saved so far. The latest version lets you close Soluto as soon as your PC has started, and also lets you search for applications by name.

Provided you're relatively ruthless about what you get rid of, you can save a

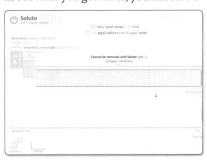

surprising amount of time and get into Windows much more quickly.

TURBOCHARGE YOUR GAMING

Game Fire (www.smartpcutilities. com) is designed to speed up your gaming session. The software, which is currently at version 1, frees up resources by shutting down any unnecessary processes and tweaks other settings to make them as game-friendly as possible. The program is very easy to use and can even defrag game files and folders on your hard disk to ensure they're arranged as efficiently as possible.

UPDATE YOUR SOFTWARE

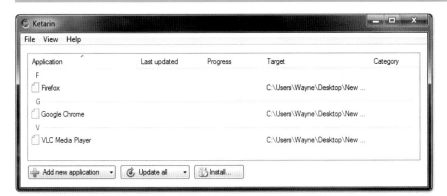

UPDATE YOUR SOFTWARE AUTOMATICALLY

Ketarin (http://ketarin.canneverbe. com) is a useful tool that monitors the download locations of your favourite installed programs and automatically fetches the latest versions as soon as they become available. You can either enter an application's name and download source manually or use a

FileHippo ID (http://filehippo.com). The program will delete any previously downloaded versions to ensure that you only ever have the latest release installed on your computer.

FIX OUT-OF-DATE DRIVERS

One way to give your PC a free performance boost and simultaneously

keep a multitude of problems at bay is to make sure you always have the latest device drivers installed.

Doing this manually can be a laborious task, but SlimDrivers (www. slimdrivers.com) saves you the effort. This new program scans your system to look for missing, broken and out-of-date drivers, then provides a direct link to the current versions.

GET THE LATEST ANTI-MALWARE SOFTWARE

Viruses, spyware and other malicious software pose a serious threat to your PC's wellbeing. Even if you never visit dodgy sites, open email attachments or click suspicious links, you can fall foul of them. It's vital to protect your system with a powerful anti-virus program, such as AVG Anti-Virus Free 2011 (http://free.avg.com) or Zillya Antivirus (http://bit.ly/zill255), which launched in 2010. See our Mini Workshop opposite to find out how to use Zillya.

DEFRAG THE REGISTRY

If you install and uninstall a lot of software, the Windows Registry is likely to become flabby over time. Simnet Registry Repair 2011 (www.simnetsoftware.com) scans and cleans the Registry, removing any unnecessary spaces, and rebuilds it to make it more efficient. The process takes only two clicks – hit Analyse Now to identify the problem areas, and then Defrag Now to make the changes.

FIX AND SPEED UP YOUR REGISTRY

Errors in the Windows Registry can cause problems such as instability, slowdowns and crashes. To prevent this happening, it's worth running the excellent Auslogics Registry Cleaner (www.auslogics.com). The latest version of the program lets you choose the sections to scan and which repairs to make, and produces a detailed report afterwards. This shows you the status of all attempted repairs and the estimated performance gain.

DETECT AND REMOVE NEW ROOTKITS

Rootkits are one of the hardest forms of malware to detect and remove. Though most decent anti-virus programs do a reasonable job of tackling the threat, it's still worth using a dedicated tool to make sure your system is truly clean. The free SpyDLLRemover (www.securityxploded.com) doesn't require installation and is very good at spotting and removing rootkit processes and suspicious DLL files. Kaspersky's TDSSKiller (http://bit.ly/kas255) can find and remove the different variations and spot other threats, too.

PROTECT YOUR MAC

While Apple computers are still far less likely to be attacked by malware than Windows systems, they aren't completely safe. To make sure your Mac doesn't pick up an infection, you can protect it using the free Sophos Anti-Virus for Mac: Home Edition (http://bit.ly/soph255). Launched in 2010, this powerful application offers all the features you'd expect in anti-virus software, including on-access and on-demand protection, heuristics and email alerts. It also detects Windows threats lurking on your Mac and prevents you from accidentally transferring them.

PREVENT SPYWARE FROM CONNECTING TO THE WEB

A good firewall will stop unauthorised software from connecting to the internet, but StreamArmor (www.securityxploded.com) provides a further layer of protection. This sophisticated tool looks at data streams (ADS) emanating from your computer and labels them as safe, dangerous, suspicious or in need of further investigation. You can sort the results

by name, threat level, content type and size, and export the report for further analysis offline. If StreamArmor finds a malicious stream, the program will let you easily remove it at source.

DEFRAGMENT YOUR HARD DISK FASTER

Defragging rearranges the contents of your hard disk so that data that is more efficiently stored side by side is kept that way. Windows comes with its own tool for the job, but we prefer to use the recently updated Defraggler (www.piriform.com/defraggler) because it offers a greater range of features, lets you target individual files and folders and can even defrag free space. The latest version has an improved engine so it defrags even faster.

FIND AND REPAIR DISK ERRORS

Problems with your hard disk can lead to program errors and data loss. Windows comes with its own built-in disk checker, but Check Disk (www.paehl.de/cms/checkdisk) is arguably better and very easy to use. You can run standard or thorough scans and quickly check if a disk has suffered some sort of corruption. The software can then repair any errors it finds.

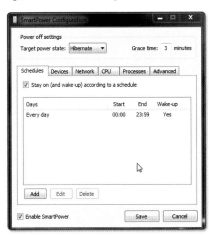

```
;[Settings]
;button=F1          Hotkey
;modifier=Shift     +=Shift ^=Ctrl !=Alt #=Win    Hotkey to turn off the screen

[Settings]
button=F1|
modifier=Shift
```

[OK]   [Cancel]

TURN YOUR SCREEN OFF WITH A KEYSTROKE

Your monitor consumes quite a lot of power, so you should always turn it off when you're not actively using your computer. If you step away for a few minutes, just flick the button to turn the screen off. You'll soon get into the habit. Alternatively, if you prefer a software solution, you can use PushMonitOff (http://bit.ly/push255). This tiny app runs in the background and shuts down the screen when you press Shift+F1 or another key combination of your choosing. Hit any key to turn your screen back on again.

MANAGE YOUR POWER-SAVING SETTINGS

Leaving your computer on overnight means you don't have to wait for it to boot up in the morning, but it also wastes a lot of electricity. Windows comes with various power-saving settings you can apply, but none of them is particularly flexible. SmartPower (http://ignatu.co.uk/SmartPower.aspx) is a useful tool that gives you much greater control, letting you schedule times for when your computer should hibernate and wake up, based on the rules you set.

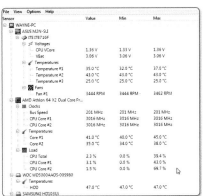

MONITOR YOUR HARD DISK

Hard-disk failure is the worst thing that can happen to your PC. These days, sudden failure is rare because hard disks come with a feature called S.M.A.R.T., which alerts you when your hard disk's health begins to deteriorate. The latest version of GSmartControl (http://bit.ly/gsmart255) produces a detailed report from your drive's S.M.A.R.T. data and also lets you run various health checks.

GET HARDWARE INFO

If your PC gets too hot, it can lead to major problems. Open Hardware Monitor (www.openhardwaremonitor.org) provides detailed information about your motherboard, processor, graphics card, and hard disk, and keeps an eye on all the built-in hardware sensors. This beta program also offers a Windows gadget that permanently displays the more important information.

Protect your PC with Zillya Antivirus

1 The main Zillya (http://bit.ly/zill255) screen shows your system status ❶, including when the program was last updated, how long it's been running and how many threats have been found. You can run a Quick Scan ❷, a Full Scan ❸ or a Custom Scan ❹. Click Updates ❺ to download the latest definition files.

2 Click Threats ❶ to view any malware detected in previous scans. You can switch between Active Threats, Quarantine and Exclusions. In Tools ❷ you can adjust Settings ❸ that let you enable and disable certain features ❹. Utilities ❺ houses Zillya's built-in Task Manager and startup manager.

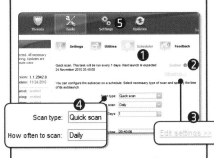

3 The program runs a Quick Scan every day. Click the Scheduler tab ❶ to turn it on or off ❷. The Edit settings link ❸ lets you configure the type of scan and frequency ❹. The Settings button ❺ at the top of the page lets you make changes to how the program behaves.

1&1 DUAL H

DOUBLE SECURITY THROUGH GEO-REDUNDANCY

No one can afford downtime of their website. This is why 1&1 Dual Hosting now offers ultimate security through geo-redundancy. This means your website exists simultaneously in two of our high-tech data centres that are in two completely different locations. If service in the first location is unexpectedly interrupted, your site will automatically continue running in the second location - without any loss of data.

OSTING

Make a fresh installer using Comodo Programs Manager

1 Once you've installed Comodo Programs Manager (http://programs-manager.comodo.com), you can create set-up files for your applications. Click the Programs button **1** to see the full list of software that can be removed or repaired. Scroll down the list to find the item you want **2** or use the search box **3** to locate it instead.

2 Check the Monitored column **1**. Anything with a Yes **2** next to it can be turned into an installer because Comodo Programs Manager will have a record of the system state before and after it was added. Assuming the application you want is suitable, click on its entry to proceed.

3 You'll be given the option to uninstall, repair or change the program **1**. Click the Make Installer button **2** and choose where you want to save the newly compressed setup file. Depending on the application, this will take a while to complete. When done, try out the installer to make sure it works properly.

FIX YOUR WEB CONNECTION

If your internet or network connection settings accidentally get changed or wiped, getting everything working again can be a nightmare. A free tool called Desktop Doctor (http://bit.ly/desk255), stops this being a problem by taking a snapshot of your settings so you can restore them should disaster strike in the future. Desktop Doctor can protect your network and Wi-Fi configuration details, Internet Explorer and Firefox bookmarks and preferences, and Windows Mail and Outlook Express settings. See our Mini Workshop opposite to find out how to use Desktop Doctor.

MAKE FRESH PROGRAM INSTALLERS

Before formatting or replacing a hard disk you need to make sure you have all the original install discs to hand, so you can quickly reinstall your existing programs. If you don't have them, Comodo Programs Manager (http://programs-manager.comodo.com) can create new self-extracting installers for you. It will include any updates and user settings, so the new installers will probably be better than the originals. See our Mini Workshop (left) to find out how to use Comodo Programs Manager.

FIND ALL YOUR SERIAL CODES

Commercial software usually requires you to enter a licence key. If you've lost this, or never had it in the first place – if the software came pre-installed on your computer, for example – then you could be in trouble. LicenseCrawler (www.klinzmann.name) will scan your system looking for serial codes for Windows, other installed Microsoft products and third-party software, and let you save

the results to a file in an encrypted or unencrypted text format for future use.

BACK UP YOUR REGISTRY

System Nucleus (www.spencerberus.com/projects.aspx) is a regularly updated collection of troubleshooting, tweaking and maintenance tools. One of its more useful features is the ability to back up copies of the Registry hives, event logs and drivers, so you can quickly restore them should you need to. Select Backup & Recovery from the menu, choose exactly what to back up and specify the location to save the files to.

CREATE A SYSTEM SNAPSHOT

Comodo Time Machine (http://bit.ly/time255) is like a more advanced version of System Restore. The program takes regular or on-demand snapshots of your entire system, recording the Windows state, the Registry, installed files and user data. In the event of Windows failing to start, you can use the software to roll things back to exactly how they were at a particular point in time.

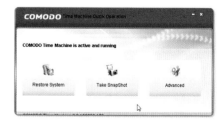

BOOST YOUR PC

MINI WORKSHOP

Boost your Wi-Fi signal using inSSIDer

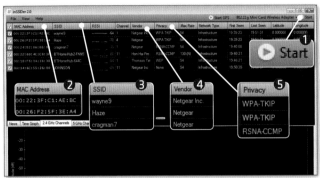

1 Download and run inSSIDer (www.metageek.net) and click the Start button **①**. The program will scan the area looking for networks in range (this can take a little while) and provide some useful information on any it finds, including their MAC addresses **②**, SSIDs **③**, the hardware manufacturer **④** and the type of encryption they're using **⑤**.

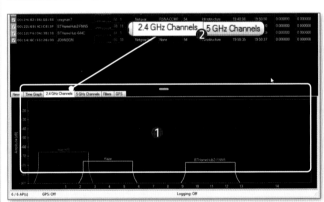

2 The graph **①** will show you the amplitude (or signal quality) of each network, and you can view the 2.4GHz and 5GHz bands **②**. In this example we're using the 2.4GHz channel, broadcasting on channel 1, as are two of our neighbours.

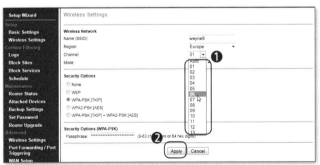

3 To avoid interference we need to pick a channel that's a reasonable distance away from those being used by other networks. In this instance, channel 6 seems ideal. Changing channels is a case of logging into the router, going into the wireless settings, picking a new choice from the drop-down menu **①** and clicking Apply **②**.

UNINSTALL UNWANTED PROGRAMS

Revo Uninstaller (www.revouninstaller.com) is an excellent alternative to the built-in Windows Add and Remove feature. Once Revo Uninstaller has uninstalled a program, it will give you the opportunity to delete any files and Registry entries that have been left behind. The latest version of the software also includes a startup manager, a junk-files cleaner and links to useful Windows tools.

REMOVE CLUTTER QUICKLY WITH SYSTEM NINJA

System Ninja (http://bit.ly/ninja255) is an impressive tool that can find and remove leftover junk files on your computer, including cached web pages, temporary files, cookies, thumbnails, Windows logs and more. The program will instantly free up valuable space and give your system a boost at the same time. You can delete everything System Ninja finds, but it's better to take a more selective approach to avoid accidentally removing something important.

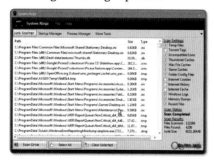

BACK UP AND SYNCHRONISE YOUR DATA

There are plenty of free third-party alternatives to Windows' built-in backup feature. One decent but lesser-known free tool is Bamboo 3 (www.haxar.com). As well as copying your data to a safe location, this program can synchronise the latest version of your files between two folders. The software's simple wizard-based interface means creating a new backup takes just a few seconds. See our Mini Workshop on the following page to find out how to use Bamboo.

DELETE UNWANTED FILES BY DATE

Windows Explorer lets you order files by the date they were modified, making it easy to locate and delete the oldest items in a folder. If you need something more advanced, give Delete Files By Date (www.deletefilesbydate.com) a try. This program lets you specify a date and time range that can be as vague or as precise as you want. You can look for files created, modified or accessed before or after a set date, in between two dates, or around a particular time of day. You can also narrow the results by file type, approximate file size and location. If you

MINI WORKSHOP

Solve PC problems using Desktop Doctor

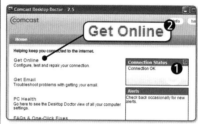

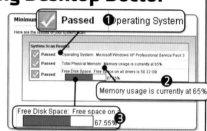

1 When you first run Desktop Doctor it will test your internet connection and display confirmation that everything is OK in the Connection Status box ❶. If any problems are reported, click the Get Online link ❷ to review your connection settings and diagnose and repair any issues.

2 Desktop Doctor lets you check that your PC's settings meet minimum requirements. Click the PC Health link on the main screen to run a system scan. This will check your operating system ❶, tell you how much memory you're using ❷ and show the amount of free disk space remaining ❸.

3 Desktop Doctor can create a snapshot of your current settings so you can easily restore them if anything goes wrong. Click the Protect & Repair Settings link on the main screen. On the Protect Settings tab, ❶ choose which settings you want the program to store by clicking the Protect button next to them ❷.

4 If you do encounter problems with any of your protected settings, click the Repair Settings tab ❶. Click the Last Protected Date drop-down menu by an entry ❷ to restore the settings to a certain date, then click Repair ❸. If the restoration doesn't work, click the Undo tab ❹ to reverse the change.

BOOST YOUR PC

wanted to delete some older archives, you could ask the program to search the C: drive for all ZIP files larger than 5MB that were created before 1 January 2007, for example.

CLEAN UP THE ADD OR REMOVE PROGRAMS LIST

Occasionally, Windows' built-in uninstaller will encounter a program that refuses to go quietly. No matter what you try, the stubborn software just won't let itself be removed, forcing you to take action and manually delete it from your system.

The problem with this approach is that the removed application's name will still appear in the programs list. To erase these ghost entries, you can use Add/Remove Program Cleaner (www.intelliadmin.com/downloads. htm). Select the problem item and hit the Remove button. Note that this tool isn't an uninstaller and should only be used as a last resort.

MOVE PROGRAMS TO A USB DRIVE

It makes sense to move programs you use only occasionally from your PC's hard disk to a USB memory drive. This will free up space on your PC, and also means you'll be able to run them from anywhere. Sites such as PortableApps (http://portableapps.com) provide pre-packaged installers for popular programs, but you can make your own using the useful tool Cameyo (www. cameyo.com). When you run the application, it will take a base snapshot of your system. Install the software you want to make portable, and Cameyo will

take another snapshot, compare the differences and generate an install-free EXE file version of the program.

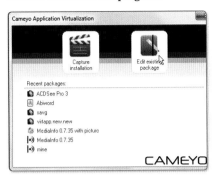

ERASE FILES PERMANENTLY

When you delete an item in Windows, only the reference to it gets removed, not the file itself. Anyone with the knowledge could retrieve it. FileKiller (http://filekiller.sourceforge.net) ensures that can't happen by overwriting the file numerous times. You choose how many passes the program makes and set the type of data to overwrite the file with.

ADD NEW FEATURES TO YOUR RECYCLE BIN

RecycleBinEx (www.fcleaner.com/recyclebinex) adds some useful features to the Windows Recycle Bin. Instead of deleting everything, you can now choose only to remove files over a certain age. The program gives you a choice of six preset options, ranging from two days to three months, and you can configure it to delete files automatically after a set number of days. RecycleBinEx also offers a selection of sorting and filtering options and lets you manage multiple bins from just one window.

MINI WORKSHOP

Back up your system with Bamboo

1 Bamboo 3 (www.haxar.com) gives you a choice of three actions. You can pair and synchronise folders ❶, back up content on your hard disk ❷ or merge and tidy up a pair of folders that no longer need to be synced ❸. To create a backup, click that option and specify the source and destination drives or folders to pair.

2 If you only want to back up certain types of file – such as music, pictures or videos – click the filters link and tick the relevant options. Click Next and give the folder pair a name. You can run the backup now (with or without selected options) ❶ or access the Advanced settings ❷.

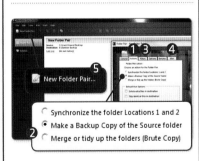

3 Click the Actions tab ❶ to switch between backing up, syncing and merging the paired folders ❷. Filters ❸ lets you specify further file types to include or exclude. You can create a backup schedule under Misc ❹. Click New Folder Pair ❺ on the toolbar to add a second source/destination.

Best free
HARD DISK TOOLS

Whether you want to clone, partition or repair your hard disk, there's a free tool available online. Here are 14 of the best

CLONE YOUR HARD DISK

Making an exact copy of your hard disk means that in the event of a problem such as a virus infection, file corruption or a complete system failure, you can restore everything to exactly the way it was. However, cloning needs to be done regularly so the copy is not out of date.

Easeus Disk Copy (www.easeus.com/disk-copy) is supplied as an ISO image that you burn to a CD using a program such as CDBurnerXP (www.cdburnerxp.se). You need two disc drives so the program can copy one to the other, either to clone the disc's contents or to restore them from a copy. The free version of HD Clone (www.hdclone.com) works similarly and can copy 40GB of data in around 74 minutes.

PARTITION YOUR HARD DISK

Partitioning a disk involves dividing the space into two or more parts that are

then treated as if they were two separate hard disks. It's a useful way to keep large files, such as videos and music, on a separate disk where they are easy to find and won't become fragmented.

Windows has its own partitioning tool for this purpose. Click Start, right-click Computer and select Manage. Under Storage in the left panel, select Disk Management, then right-click the disk and select Shrink Volume. This turns the free space at the end of the disk into a new drive. You can now format this and use it like a regular disk. Note that this function isn't available in Windows XP.

If you're after a more sophisticated partitioning tool, there are powerful free programs available that offer additional features. Two of the best are Partition Wizard (www.partitionwizard.com) and Easeus Partition Master (www.partition-tool.com/personal.htm).

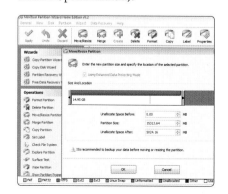

BACK UP THE DATA ON YOUR HARD DISK

Cloning your hard disk is a useful way to back it up to protect against system failure, but individual file and folder backups help you safeguard your documents, photos, videos and other files in the event of a PC disaster.

A backup feature is built into Windows 7 so if a problem occurs, you can simply right-click on a file or folder and choose the option to 'Restore previous versions'. However, a disk fault can destroy backups as well as the originals, so it's essential to use either an external disk or an online service.

GFI Backup (www.gfi.com/backup-hm) is an excellent free tool that uses a wizard to guide you through the process of backing up files to CD, DVD, Blu-ray, USB memory sticks and more. Online storage service MozyHome (http://mozy.co.uk) gives you 2GB of backup space for free so is worth signing up for.

COMPRESS YOUR HARD DISK

If you're running short of disk space, you can compress the disk contents so the files occupy less space. Click Start, Computer, right-click the disk and choose Properties, then tick the box to compress the drive. Be warned, though, that this has the unfortunate side effect of making it harder to recover from disk faults and to restore lost files.

A better way to save space is to right-click a folder, choose Properties, then Advanced, and select the option 'Compress contents to save disk space'. You should create backups to save elsewhere in case there are problems.

You can right-click a file or folder and choose Send To, then Compressed (zipped) Folder to create a zip file, but the free tools IZArc (www.izarc.org) and PeaZip (http://peazip.sourceforge.net) will compress your files to an even smaller size.

DEFRAGMENT YOUR HARD DISK

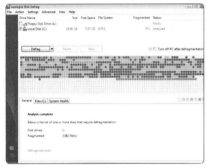

Over time, files on your hard disk can become split into small fragments, so Windows automatically defragments them to prevent your PC from slowing down. However, third-party tools do a better job and can even boost the performance of your PC a little.

Auslogics' Disk Defrag (www.auslogics.com/en/software/disk-defrag) is one of the best options and it's also available as a screensaver, which means that it can optimise your hard disk whenever your PC is idle.

Equally good is IObit Smart Defrag (www.iobit.com), which offers three different optimisation methods and can also work while your PC is idle. You can set how long the program should wait before it begins defragmentation and stop the process if you're using the PC for something important.

INCREASE YOUR HARD DISK SPACE

If you don't mind splashing out, the best way to increase the disk space on your PC is to add a USB disk drive. Shop around online for the best deals because it's possible to get a 1TB (1,000GB) drive for as little as £50 from electronics stores such as Scan (www.scan.co.uk). Recommended brands include Freecom (www.freecom.com) and Buffalo (www.buffalo-technology.com).

Alternatively, you can sign up for Windows Live SkyDrive (http://skydrive.live.com), which provides 25GB of online storage for free. You can upload files you rarely use but don't want to lose, then delete them from your hard disk to free up extra space.

Some online storage services, such as ADrive (www.adrive.com), provide WebDAV (Web-based Distributed Authoring and Versioning) access, which lets you add their space as if it were an extra hard disk attached to your computer. Although it's a bit slow, WebDAV makes it very easy to copy files from your PC to the web and back.

CHECK YOUR HARD DISK FOR ERRORS

It's always a good idea to check your hard disk for errors after a program crashes and before you install new software or Windows updates. Click Start, Computer, right-click the disk and select Properties. Click Check Now on the Tools tab and tick the option 'Automatically fix file system errors'. It's only necessary to select the option to scan for bad sectors once or twice a year, though, even if you regularly install new software.

Most hard disk manufacturers, including Seagate (www.seagate.com) and Western Digital (www.wdc.com), provide free tools for checking your hard disk, but an alternative is to get S.M.A.R.T. (self-monitoring, analysis and reporting technology). All modern drives contain S.M.A.R.T. and, if you install PassMark DiskCheckup (www.passmark.com), you'll be able to view your disk's health information at a glance – everything from its temperature to the time it takes to start up. In this way, you'll get fair warning of when your hard disk might fail so you can replace it before that happens.

How to
SAVE MONEY BY CUTTING YOUR PC'S ENERGY

Top tips to help you save cash by reducing your PC's power usage

With energy prices rocketing, it makes sense to cut back your electricity usage where possible. Your PC probably consumes quite a bit of power, but you don't have to limit the time you spend on it to make savings. By making some basic tweaks and installing some free software, you can easily reduce the amount of energy your computer consumes and save money every time you use your PC. Here are our suggestions.

TURN OFF YOUR MONITOR

Flat-screen displays use far less electricity than old CRT models but they also tend to be larger. As a result, there's no great energy-saving difference, particularly if you have a multi-monitor setup. Get into the habit of flicking the off switch every time you step away from your PC.

SAY NO TO SCREENSAVERS

Years ago, screensavers served an important purpose. They literally saved your screen from the danger of phosphor burn-in – a permanent still image that could get burned into your screen if left to display continuously over a long period of time. That's not a problem for modern monitors, though. The only thing screensavers do these days, aside from look pretty, is waste electricity by keeping your processor and graphics card working unnecessarily. Turn them off by right-clicking a blank area of your Desktop and selecting Properties or Personalize.

USE GRANOLA TO LOWER YOUR ELECTRICITY BILL

Granola (http://grano.la) is a clever utility that makes use of DVFS (dynamic voltage and frequency settings) to regulate your processor's speed and energy consumption intelligently. When you use your computer, the processor will function pretty much as normal. During idle moments, however, Granola will reduce the power to it, saving electricity. Over time, these savings can become significant.

Granola reduces the power your PC uses when it's idle

You simply open the program to see exactly how much you've saved so far in kilowatts, money, carbon dioxide consumption and as an overall percentage. The program will also show you how many trees you and the Granola community have offset just by using the software. If you create an account, you can link multiple computers to it, and monitor the cumulative savings. You can track up to five machines free of charge.

TAKE CONTROL OVER YOUR PC'S POWER SETTINGS

Edison (www.verdiem.com/edison) lets you create power plans for different times of the day. For example, you can have your computer running at maximum efficiency during working hours, but then have more energy-saving features kick in during the evening.

You can use the program's slider to change the settings or you can customise them manually. Your estimated savings will be shown in the panel below the slider. You can change your working hours and configure the price you pay for your electricity, so the estimated savings are always accurate.

Customise your computer's energy usage throughout the day by using Edison

HIBERNATE IT

Hibernation is a power-saving option designed primarily for laptops. When a PC goes into this mode, everything in the memory is copied to a file called Hiberfil.sys and the computer is powered down. When you switch your PC back on again, Windows loads this file straight into memory, without performing any boot checks, so everything starts up much faster.

To enable the feature on a desktop PC running Windows XP, click the Hibernate tab in Power Options, tick Enable Hibernation and click Apply. To enter Hibernation manually, go to Start and select Shut Down. Hold Shift and the Standby entry will change to Hibernate.

In Windows 7, click Start and type cmd, then hit Ctrl+Shift+Enter to open a command prompt window with administration rights. Type powercfg /hibernate on and hit Enter. If there's no Hibernate option visible in the Shutdown menu, click Start, type 'power options' (without the quotes) and hit Enter. Click the 'Change when the computer sleeps' link on the left and then click 'Change advanced power settings'. Click the plus sign next to Sleep to expand the entry, and change the 'Allow hybrid sleep' option to Off.

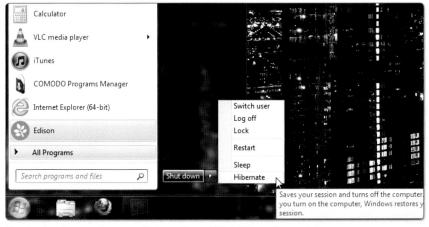

If you're stepping away from your PC for a while, put it into Hibernation mode to save energy

MINI WORKSHOP

Tweak Windows 7's power settings

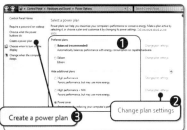

1 It's easy to configure the various Windows power plans. Click Start, type 'power options' (without the quotes) into the box and hit Enter. You can select any of the available plans ❶, customise a plan's settings to suit your requirements ❷ or create a bespoke one from scratch ❸.

2 When editing a plan, you have two options – you can set how long your PC needs to be idle before the display is automatically turned off ❶ and the computer is put to sleep ❷. This can be anything from one minute to never. Click 'Change advanced power settings' ❸ to further personalise the plan.

3 Make sure the plan you want is selected ❶, then open each setting by clicking the plus sign next to it ❷. Make the adjustments you need. Certain options, such as the Wireless Adapter Settings ❸, are probably best left at maximum performance. Click Apply ❹ to save the changes.

Group test

DNS SERVERS

Can changing your DNS server boost the speed and security of your internet connection? We test three free packages to find out

Few people know or care about the Domain Name System (DNS), but it's a core part of the internet. Usually hosted by your ISP, this server receives the URL you type into your browser (such as www.google.co.uk) and converts it to the IP address (such as 72.14.204.103) needed to deliver the pages to your browser.

When you subscribe to your ISP, the setup procedure will automatically tell your PC where to find your ISP's

DNS servers. However, other DNS services are available and there's nothing to stop you using a different one. Some DNS servers claim to be quicker at converting URLs to IP addresses, for example, while others offer extra security features that can help protect you from malicious websites.

We've tested three of the best alternative DNS servers to see how much of an impact they make on your surfing speed and whether they can make your web browsing safer.

OpenDNS

★★★★★

www.opendns.com

FEATURES ★★★★★ PERFORMANCE ★★★★★ EASE OF USE ★★★★☆

There are two ways to use OpenDNS: you can simply change the addresses of the DNS servers your computer or router use to the ones OpenDNS provides; or you can create an account with the service and access a wide range of additional features. These extra features make the website more complex than some rival services, but it's not too difficult to find the information you need to get it set up.

The Windows instructions cover every version from 98 up to Windows 7, with screenshots to help you every step of the way. There are also instructions for setting up 19 brands of router, again with step-by-step guides and screenshots. Interestingly, the instructions work just as well if you use them to set up the other two services on test opposite.

Once you've changed DNS servers and restarted Windows, your browser will use them instead of your ISP's to deliver web pages. OpenDNS responds to URLs very quickly and was the fastest on test. There wasn't much of a difference between the three services, and you

won't notice huge differences in web-browsing speed, but any speed boost, however small, has to be a good thing.

The main benefit of OpenDNS, though, is its extra features. There are four levels of content filters to block adult or other unsuitable content, which is ideal if you have a home network where children surf the web with minimal supervision. You can also configure a custom level of filtering, where you choose what content to allow and block. OpenDNS also offers phishing and malware

protection, web statistics, logs (so you can see which sites have been accessed), auto-correction of typing errors when entering web addresses and more.

OUR VERDICT

OpenDNS came top in our tests, improving on our ISP's speed by a small but significant margin. It also has a range of features that can protect your PC and your family from malicious websites, whether they're hosting malware or dubious content. It's a fantastic free service and is strongly recommended.

GOLD

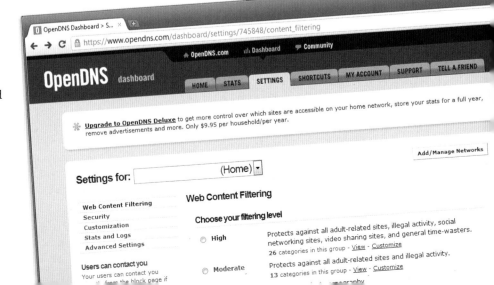

SAVE MONEY ONLINE

ClearCloud

★★★★☆

www.clearclouddns.com

FEATURES ★★★☆☆ **PERFORMANCE** ★★★★★ **EASE OF USE** ★★★★★

ClearCloud stands out from the other services here because of its clarity, simplicity and ease of use. If you're not a technical expert and aren't familiar with the ins and outs of networking, the ClearCloud website is the easiest to use. Even better is the simple downloadable tool that lets you switch from your current DNS servers to ClearCloud's and back again whenever you like. Turning ClearCloud on and off with a single mouse click is an excellent feature.

Not everyone wants to install software and have it constantly running, though, so manual setup instructions for Windows 7, Vista and XP are also provided, which requires no software. These also tell you how to put things back as they were, should you need to. There are detailed instructions on how to set up the service on popular routers too, including devices made by Asus, Belkin, Linksys, Netgear and Netcomm. The guidelines aren't quite as helpful as those from OpenDNS, but they're much better than Google's.

The company behind ClearCloud is Sunbelt, which produces anti-virus, anti-spyware and other security software. This security know-how is put to good use with ClearCloud – every web address your computer requests is checked against a blacklist, and you're warned if you're about to visit a malicious site. Modern web browsers do this too, but there's no harm in adding this extra layer of security.

It doesn't seem to slow the system down, though, and in fact we found the ClearCloud DNS servers to be slightly faster than Google's, which don't do any checking at all.

OUR VERDICT

ClearCloud has clear setup instructions, and also offers a simple application that will do all the installation for you if you wish. It provides protection against malicious websites and is fast. However, although its performance was slightly better than Google's, it wasn't quite as good as OpenDNS's.

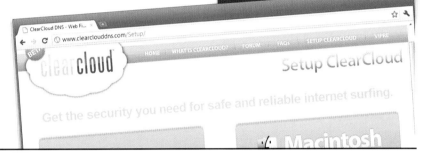

HOW TO SET THE DNS SERVER

When you enter a URL such as www. bbc.co.uk into your browser, it sends a request to a DNS server to convert it into an IP address, such as 212.58.246.93. If no DNS server has been set in Windows, then the router provides one; if the router doesn't have one set, the ISP's is used. So to avoid using the ISP's DNS server, you simply set it on either your PC or router.

Setting it on your PC is easy, but it will apply only to that machine. Set it on the router, however, and every connected computer in your home will use it automatically. It's a bit harder to do, though, and you need to know your router's password.

To set the DNS server in Windows 7 and Vista, click Start, type 'Network' (without the quotes) and click 'Network and Sharing Center'. Listed under Active Networks is your home network, and on the right is a link called Local Area Connection or View Status. Click it and click Properties in the next window. Select Internet Protocol Version 4 and click Properties. Select 'Use the following DNS server

addresses' and, for OpenDNS, enter 208.67.222.222 and 208.67.220.220 into the boxes (substitute the server addresses below for ClearCloud or Google Public DNS if you're using those services). Close the dialog boxes and restart Windows.

To configure the DNS server on most routers, you simply enter the router's IP address into the address bar of a web browser – it will be 192.168.2.1 or something similar, so check the documentation. You might then need to enter a username and password to access the settings. Once you're in, head for the WAN section and then DNS. As with Windows, there are boxes to enter the DNS server addresses. There are always two – a primary and a secondary DNS server.

WHAT SERVER ADDRESSES DO I NEED?

OpenDNS	ClearCloud	Google Public DNS
208.67.222.222	74.118.212.1	8.8.8.8
208.67.220.220	74.118.212.2	8.8.4.4

Google Public DNS

★★★☆☆

http://code.google.com/speed/public-dns

FEATURES ★★☆☆☆ **PERFORMANCE** ★★★★☆ **EASE OF USE** ★★★★☆

Google's DNS service provides a pair of domain name servers with easy-to-remember addresses. Configuration instructions are provided for Windows 7 and Vista, but XP users might struggle as it's a slightly different procedure. We'd recommend non-technical Windows XP users follow the excellent OpenDNS or ClearCloud instructions, but substitute Google's numbers in the final step.

The main advantages of Google's DNS servers over your ISP's are speed and reliability. The system is designed for high performance, using smart caches, load balancing and other highly technical methods to increase the speed.

It certainly seemed fast in our tests, but wasn't quite as speedy as OpenDNS and ClearCloud, even though those two services run extra features that must slow down performance. However,

complex web pages with multiple components loaded more quickly than with our standard ISP settings.

Unlike its two rivals, Google doesn't filter requested websites, which some people will see as a positive feature. Adults who don't share their computer may wish to have no restrictions placed on their web access, while parents will obviously approve of their children being sheltered from mature content. However, on the downside, the service won't warn you if you try to visit websites that are known to harbour malware or phishing scams.

This is a limitation but not a serious one, because modern web browsers such as Internet Explorer and Firefox check URLs anyway.

OUR VERDICT

Google's DNS servers don't offer extra features, just extra performance. If you don't want any restrictions on what sites you access, it's a great way to boost browsing speed. Drive-by browser-based spyware is on the increase, however, so be sure to get this kind of protection from elsewhere.

SPEED TEST RESULTS

To measure the performance of the DNS servers, we sent nine typical web-browsing queries to each one and recorded how long they took to respond. The graph below shows the average speed in milliseconds.

To give you an idea of how they compare to a British ISP's DNS servers, we included BT in the test. Your own ISP's DNS servers may be better or worse than BT's, so the benefits for your connection may vary. Timings are also affected by the time of day, internet congestion and so on, so these aren't absolute results.

Our ISP was four times slower than the three services on test, but we're talking milliseconds here. The DNS servers won't speed up file downloads, but compared to your ISP they might shave off a few fractions of a second every time you visit a web page. As a result, clicking web links may feel more responsive.

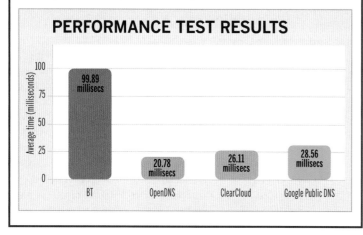

PERFORMANCE TEST RESULTS

Average time (milliseconds)

BT	99.89 millisecs
OpenDNS	20.78 millisecs
ClearCloud	26.11 millisecs
Google Public DNS	28.56 millisecs

OVERALL VERDICT

In our tests, all three DNS servers were around four times faster than our ISP's. Although only milliseconds might be saved every time you click, this will benefit you in the long term. You may also find a bigger boost at peak times, when your local ISP is bogged down with lots of users.

If the speed differences aren't enough to sell it to you, it's still worth considering switching services for some of the extra features. If it's security you're after, ClearCloud offers malware and phishing protection, with a respected security company behind it. This may offer the edge over Google's Bronze Award-winning service, or that of your current ISP. If you want it all, however, you should opt for OpenDNS. This offers similar malware and phishing protection to ClearCloud, but adds web filtering on top. It was also the fastest in our tests, so it deserves our Gold Award.

However, if you don't want to have your web experience filtered before it reaches your web browser, Google's service is well worth considering. It remained significantly faster than our ISP but doesn't interfere with the information coming through, so it's the ideal choice if you're looking for pure, unadulterated internet content without any filters or blocks.

BOOST YOUR PC

Make your anti-virus
FASTER & BETTER

Is your anti-virus program slowing down your system? We suggest six expert ways to speed up your scans and make them more effective

RUN SCANS IN SAFE MODE

Because programs, drivers and non-essential system files are automatically disabled in Windows' Safe Mode, your anti-virus software will scan more quickly and thoroughly when it's in this state. It's also easier to remove viruses, spyware and other malicious files that haven't been given the chance to load.

To enter Safe Mode, restart your computer and press F8 repeatedly to access the Windows Advanced Options Menu. Choose Safe Mode, click Administrator and enter your password if needed. Then run your anti-virus program as normal.

SCAN INDIVIDUAL FOLDERS

Although it's advisable to run a full system scan on a regular basis, you can save time in the interim by checking specific folders for viruses. This is useful if, for example, you've just downloaded lots of new songs to your Music folder and want to ensure the files are clean and free of malware.

Most anti-virus programs add a scanning option to your right-click menu, or you can select the folder(s) to scan from within the software. In AVG Anti-Virus Free Edition 2011 (http://free.avg.com), click the Tools menu and choose 'Scan selected folder'. In Avast

Free Antivirus 6 (www.avast.com), click Scan Computer, then click the Start button next to 'Select folder to scan'.

SCHEDULE SCANS DURING IDLE TIME

If your anti-virus program keeps slowing down your system, try shifting the scan to a time when you're not using your PC.

To schedule a scan in AVG, click the Tools menu, select 'Advanced settings', double-click Schedules and choose 'Scheduled scan'. Select 'Enable this task', choose the time and date to run the scan, and then specify 'How to scan' and 'What to scan' on the relevant tabs.

In Avast, click the 'More details' link next to a scan, click Settings, select Scheduling and specify your options.

EXCLUDE SPECIFIC FOLDERS FROM SCANS

Another way to speed up your anti-virus tool is to exclude 'low-risk' folders from your scans. According to an article at PC-tips website How-To Geek (http://bit.ly/custom262), skipping folders such as your photo library (provided all the images have come from your camera) and Windows Update folders can improve the performance of your security software.

To choose folders to exclude in AVG, go to 'Advanced settings', double-click 'Resident Shield' and select 'Excluded Items'. In Avast, go into the Settings for a scan and click Exclusions.

Be aware, however, that because malware can infect any area of your PC, you exclude folders at your own risk.

CUSTOMISE SCAN SETTINGS

By default, anti-virus programs are set up to give the average PC user the best balance between security and performance. However, if you find your scans are too slow, you can customise the software to speed it up. However, making it faster may also make it less efficient at identifying hidden malware.

In AVG, go into 'Advanced settings', double-click Scans and click 'Whole computer scan'. Here you can disable various options to improve performance and use the slider bar to adjust the scanning speed. The 'User sensitive' setting uses minimal system resources while you're working and switches to a high-priority mode when your PC is idle. In Avast, you can create a custom scan using the settings of your choice.

CHANGE UPDATE SETTINGS

If your anti-virus program's automatic updates are affecting the performance of your PC, you can run them less often. To do this in Avast, click Settings, then Updates. Scroll down to Details and type how long you want to leave between updates in the 'Auto-update interval' box.

AVG doesn't let you change its update frequency, but you can run a manual update to override the automatic one by right-clicking the System Tray icon and selecting 'Update now'.

PHOTO TIPS

Recover lost photos for free

If you've accidentally deleted valuable images from your PC or camera, don't despair. Here are seven free ways to get your precious pictures back

Most of us have experienced that heart-stopping moment when we realise we've accidentally deleted an important file. Erasing a personal photo can be particularly traumatic because pictures often have sentimental value and – unlike music or software – you can't simply download them again. Similarly, a corrupt memory card in your camera may mean a whole holiday's snaps are lost forever. Thankfully, there are a number of steps you can take to recover lost photos.

CHECK YOUR RECYCLE BIN
It sounds obvious, but before you start panicking over missing photos, it's worth looking in the Recycle Bin. If you haven't emptied it for a while, click the Date Deleted column to reorganise its contents with the most recently deleted items at the top. To rescue a picture from the Bin, right-click the file and select Restore. If you can't see your deleted photo, try showing hidden files by going to Tools, Folder Options, View and selecting 'Show hidden files, folders and drives'.

SEARCH YOUR HARD DISK
There's a chance the the 'hot ma' have been moved to a different folder rather than deleted from your PC. Try running the Windows search tool for 'Pictures and Photos' or use a Desktop search program such as Google Desktop (http://desktop.google.com). Obviously, the more you can remember of the file name the better, but you can always sort results by date modified and try searching by file extension, such as 'jpg', to make things easier. Generally, you should only need to search your My Documents folder and perhaps your Desktop (if it's messy).

RUN THE RECUVA WIZARD
Recuva (www.piriform.com/recuva), which is from the same software stable as CCleaner, is an essential tool to have on your PC. This powerful free data-recovery program offers a dedicated 'wizard' for rescuing lost images, which makes the entire process pleasantly painless. It also has a Deep Scan mode for more comprehensive image scouring. You can retrieve files that have been deleted from your camera's memory card, your PC's My Documents folder, Recycle Bin and other locations, and restore them to the destination of your choice.

There's also a portable version of Recuva (http://bit.ly/recuva259). This requires no installation so it won't overwrite any precious data when you run it. See our Mini Workshop (right) to find out how to use Recuva.

TRY PC INSPECTOR SMART RECOVERY
If Recuva can't find your lost photos, try PC Inspector Smart Recovery 4.5 (http://bit.ly/pcinspector259). This excellent free program will restore deleted and corrupted images from most memory cards, as well as your hard disk and USB drive. The software supports a wide range of image and movie file formats, and 'mally' di-plays thousands of JPEGs in its search results to help y u quickly identify the pictures you're after. Like Recuva, PC Inspector Smart Recovery offers both a fast-scanning mode and a deeper, much slower Intensive mode and will restore pictures to the destination of your choice.

RESCUE PHOTOS FROM A DAMAGED DISC
Storing your pictures on a CD or DVD is a great way to archive them, but if the disc gets damaged, you're in trouble. Help is at hand from the free CD Recovery Toolbox (http://bit.ly/cdrec250). It's designed for retrieving unreadable files from damaged CDs and DVDs. Once you've installed the program, simply select the drive you want to restore from, choose the files you want to rescue and click Save.

CHECK ONLINE ACCOUNTS FOR BACKUPS
If you've uploaded pictures to Facebook (www.facebook.com), Flickr (www.flickr.com) or photo-printing services such as PhotoBox (www.photobox.co.uk), you've effectively created backup copies in the process. If you've accidentally deleted an old photo from your hard disk or camera, it's worth checking your online accounts to see if you've previously uploaded it. You might not be able to download it at the original resolution, but at least you'll have a version of the image.

ESSENTIAL RECOVERY TIPS
■ If you want to rescue lost photos, don't take any more! Any pictures that you save to your camera's memory card could overwrite your lost images, reducing your chance of getting them back.
■ Save your restored photos to a different drive on your PC or, if possible, to a USB memory stick. This will prevent you from overwriting any other images you want to save.
■ Keep a 'recovery toolkit' of programs such as Recuva and Zero Assumption Recovery (see above) stored on a USB drive so they're ready to run if you ever accidentally delete a photo.
■ If your memory card has a write-protect switch, flick it to 'on' so that the data on it can't be overwritten.
■ If nothing works, try a data-recovery company such as Kroll Ontrack (www.ontrackdatarecovery.co.uk). Prices vary according to the type of data loss, but you can request a quote online.

GIVE ZERO ASSUMPTION RECOVERY A GO
Zero Assumption Recovery, or ZAR, (www.z-a-recovery.com) is another useful tool for rescuing deleted images. The program is particularly good at retrieving photos from corrupt and accidentally formatted memory cards, and supports a wide range of image formats. The software lets you preview each picture before you restore it, to save you rescuing unwanted files. Recovering images using ZAR is completely free, but the program does include some other features that require registration.

Best free PHOTO SOFTWARE

30 TOP PROGRAMS

Why pay for commercial photo software when there are lots of superb programs available for free? Here are 30 of the best applications for editing, organising and applying effects to your images

IMAGE EDITORS

VIRTUALSTUDIO

www.optikvervelabs.com
REQUIREMENTS Windows XP/Vista/7
FILE SIZE 3.5MB

VirtualStudio is a well-designed photo editor that lets you fix and enhance your images, and apply a range of VirtualPhotographer filters. There are lots of different effects on offer, including Sixties Slide, which gives a tint that emulates old-fashioned colour film, Moonlit, which makes the photo look like it was taken at night, and ShoeBox, which makes it look like a negative.

There's also a film option that mimics old film stocks and makes photos look like they were taken at different shutter speeds. With its unique editing features, VirtualStudio is great fun to play around with.

CHASYS DRAW IES

www.chachaslab.com
REQUIREMENTS Windows XP/Vista/7
FILE SIZE 12.1MB

Chasys Draw IES is actually a suite of applications, which include a drawing, painting and photo-editing program, an image viewer, a RAW editor and a conversion tool. The main editor (Artist) offers an array of useful features, such as support for layers, a cloning brush, pen and path selection, levels, curves and a range of powerful effects and filters. The software also supports Photoshop plug-ins. While having lots of tool windows open can clutter up some image editors, in this one they are kept transparent until required, so nothing gets obscured.

PAINT.NET

www.getpaint.net
REQUIREMENTS Windows XP/Vista/7
FILE SIZE 3.5MB

Paint.NET is one of the most user-friendly image editors, with an intuitive tabbed interface that lets you quickly jump between multiple open photos with ease. The software offers advanced

features such as layers, levels and curves, and has a decent collection of filters and effects. Paint.NET also supports third-party plug-ins, which add further functionality to the program. The most recent release fixed a lot of long-standing bugs and improved the image editor's performance, as well as adding integration with right-click (context) menus in Windows. An equally powerful image-editing alternative is GIMP (www. gimp.org), but Paint.NET is much more straightforward to use.

FOTOGRAFIX

http://lmadhavan.com/software
REQUIREMENTS Windows XP/Vista/7
FILE SIZE 356KB

Despite its small size, Fotografix is a decent – and fast – image editor with support for layers, layer masks and levels. You can blur and sharpen images, add noise and apply filters such as Solarize and Night Vision. Fotografix also supports scripts and the default collection lets you add vignettes (lighting changes), stencilled text and rubber stamps to your pictures, as well as give your images a sepia tint.

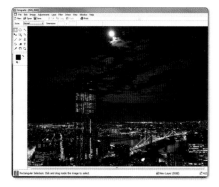

PHOTO ORGANISERS

PICASA

http://picasa.google.com
REQUIREMENTS Windows XP/Vista/7,
Mac OS X
FILE SIZE 9MB

Google's popular photo-management software covers pretty much everything you could want to do with your pictures, from organising images by various criteria to fixing and enhancing shots. Picasa also boasts a powerful facial-recognition feature for automatically identifying people in your pictures, and lets you geo-tag images in Google Earth and Maps so you can plot where they were taken on a map. The latest version of the program lets you simultaneously upload multiple albums to Picasa Web Albums and enhance photos using online editor Picnik (www.picnik.com).

There's also a clever new feature called Face Movie, which lets you create a video

Make a Face Movie using Picasa

1 Launch Picasa (http://picasa.google.com) and select photos of the person you want to use in your video by dragging them into the Photo Tray in the bottom-left corner of the screen ❶. You can save time by choosing the person's album in the People folder ❷.

2 Now you can either click the Create Face Movie button (fourth button along, next to the person's profile picture in the People folder) ❶ or click the Create menu ❷, go to Video and choose 'From Faces in Selection' ❸. Either method will launch the Video Maker.

3 Your Face Movie will now be generated. In the left-hand panel, you can change the style of the transitions between photos ❶, the length of time to display each slide ❷ and the degree of overlap ❸. Click Create Video ❹ to produce and save your Face Movie.

from images of a particular person, keeping their face centred and in focus as the photos transition from one to the next. See our Mini Workshop (left) to find out how to use Face Movie.

PICAJET FREE
www.picajet.com
REQUIREMENTS Windows XP/Vista/7
FILE SIZE 4.8MB
PicaJet Free is a powerful photo manager that can automatically organise and tag your image collection, and import media from a variety of devices, including digital cameras and scanners, as well as other programs. You can sort photos by various criteria, including who's in them and where they were taken. The program can also batch-resize and convert groups of pictures, fix common problems and create web photo galleries. See our Mini Workshop opposite to find out how to organise your photos with PicaJet Free.

ADEBIS PHOTO SORTER
www.adebis.com
REQUIREMENTS Windows XP/Vista/7
FILE SIZE 638KB
Manually organising a really messy photo collection can take ages, but

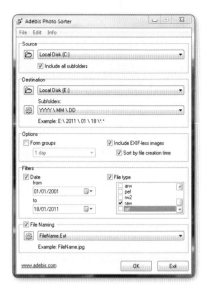

fortunately, there's a quick and easy solution that's available for free from the web. Simply fire up Photo Sorter, select a drive or folder, and the program will copy your images into chronological sub-folders based on their EXIF data (the information stored by your camera in every shot you take). You can filter your collection by date and format, and also batch-rename images.

When Adebis Photo Sorter has finished its job, you'll then need to delete the original photos manually if you want to avoid having a hard disk full of duplicate images.

IMAGE VIEWERS

FIRST IMPRESSION
www.utilhaven.com/fi
REQUIREMENTS Windows XP/Vista/7
FILE SIZE 234KB
This lightweight application displays your photos full size and full screen. You can click and drag your way around large images, and zoom in and out using the plus and minus keys. Right-click anywhere in First Impression to display the menu and flip or rotate the current photo, change the interpolation mode

(the algorithm that is used when an image is scaled or rotated) and set the photo as your Desktop wallpaper.

FASTSTONE IMAGE VIEWER
www.faststone.org
REQUIREMENTS Windows XP/Vista/7
FILE SIZE 5.1MB
FastStone Image Viewer lets you browse thumbnails of all your images and videos in an Explorer-style interface. You can

PHOTO TIPS

view photos in a slideshow or an image strip, compare up to four shots side by side and fix flaws and apply effects.

Among the many features on offer are brushes to clone, heal and remove red-eye; level and curve tools; and a drawing board to add captions, annotations and shapes to photos. Double-click an image to view it full screen, then move your mouse to one of the outer edges to access various tools and information.

IRFANVIEW
www.irfanview.com
REQUIREMENTS Windows XP/Vista/7
FILE SIZE 1.4MB
IrfanView is a massively popular image viewer, and it's not hard to see why. Despite its small file size, the program is

fast, easy to use and efficient, and offers lots of powerful features. IrfanView can display thumbnails of images in a folder, show photos full screen, set pictures as wallpaper, create a panorama or a slideshow, add effects, borders or frames and perform many more functions. The software also supports Photoshop filters so you can add additional features.

PHOTO-SHARING TOOLS

PIXUM PHOTO BOOK
www.pixum.co.uk/photo-book-software.html
REQUIREMENTS Windows XP/Vista/7, Mac OS X, Linux
FILE SIZE 77.6MB
You don't always want to have to power up your computer or go online to view your images. The modern equivalent of the family album is the photo book – a bespoke collection of your favourite photos, printed and bound in a stylish hard- or soft-cover volume.

Pixum's software lets you select a type of book, then builds the album from the photographs that you supply. You can resize the images, swap them for different shots, move pictures around, choose a different layout, add captions and much more. Or, if you prefer, you can build a photo book from scratch and have complete control over its design.

When you've finished, you can purchase your book(s). Prices start from £5.99 (plus P&P) for a small booklet.

VISUAL LIGHTBOX JS
http://visuallightbox.com
REQUIREMENTS Windows XP/Vista/7, Mac OS X
FILE SIZE 11.3MB

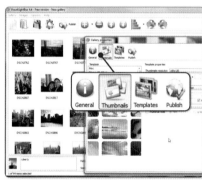

If you want to share photos online, this wizard-based program can transform a collection of photos into a stylish HTML gallery. You simply drag images or folders to the program window or click the Add button and browse for them. You can reorder, rotate and rename the pictures, select a template and enable or disable various features. Visual LightBox JS then lets you click Publish to open the gallery in your browser.

WINDOWS LIVE PHOTO GALLERY
http://bit.ly/windows259
REQUIREMENTS Windows Vista/7
FILE SIZE 1.22MB (installer)
Microsoft's revamped imaging software is packed with impressive features,

MINI WORKSHOP

Organise photos with PicaJet Free

Create Categories from Folders Names

1 Install and run PicaJet Free (www.picajet.com) and the wizard will guide you through the process of organising your images. You can scan files and folders or import an existing database. Select the former option, then choose the folders to scan ❶. You can have the program generate categories from the folder names ❷.

2 PicaJet Free will now import your images. When it's finished, it will display rows of thumbnails ❶. If you didn't ask the program to assign categories, you can create some now. Click the 'Add new category' button ❷ to create a new folder. Give it a name and drag the relevant images to it.

3 Double-click a photo to view it. Right-click and select Fix Image to adjust brightness/contrast, hue/saturation and other settings ❶. Select 'Before and After' ❷ to see the results of your changes. The right-click menu also has a Quick Edit option to auto-fix photos.

1. Install and run Tintii (www.indii. org), click the Open button ❶ and browse for the picture to which you want to apply effects. The program will display a black-and-white preview image ❷. To reintroduce some colour, click one or more of the thumbnails on the right ❸. The preview will update instantly to show the results.

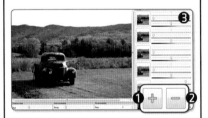

2. Click the plus sign ❶ to get more colour variations to play around with. Click the minus sign ❷ to reduce the number of available options. The three slider bars next to each thumbnail ❸ let you play around with the hue, saturation and brightness of the colour in the photo.

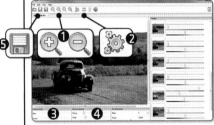

3. Use the magnifying glass icons ❶ to zoom in and out of the picture. The cogs icon ❷ restores the defaults, removing any additional colour thumbnails. Use the Channel Mixer ❸ to fine-tune the colours, and the Post and Pre-processing options ❹ to make additional changes. When you've finished, click Save ❺.

especially when it comes to sharing pictures. You can instantly upload photos and videos to Facebook, Flickr and YouTube, as well as Microsoft's SkyDrive online storage service.

Facial recognition has been improved, so people in your photos are identified automatically, which saves you having to tag your images manually. You can also use Windows Live Photo Gallery to merge similar shots into a single image.

PHOTO-EFFECTS TOOLS

TINTII
www.indii.org/software/tintii
REQUIREMENTS Windows XP/Vista/7, Mac OS X or Linux
FILE SIZE 7.8MB

Colour popping (or selective colouring) is the process of adding a spot of colour to a greyscale picture to produce eye-catching results. Open a colour photograph in Tintii and the program will turn it into a greyscale image and create four layers of colour. Select one or more of these layers to re-introduce the coloured elements. For example, you could highlight individual flowers in a monochrome picture of a garden or someone's eyes and lips in a portrait. See our Mini Workshop (left) to find out how to get the most from Tintii.

PHOTOFILTRE
http://photofiltre.en.softonic.com
REQUIREMENTS Windows XP/Vista/7
FILE SIZE 1.88MB

As well as offering all the usual editing features, this excellent photo-retouching tool contains more than 100 filters and adjustment options that let you create a variety of interesting effects. You can make a photo look like a painting, for example, add frames and textures, and even make a daytime shot look as if it was taken at night.

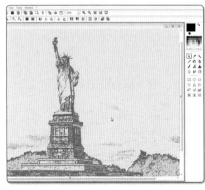

ALAMOON COLOR ENHANCER
www.alamoon.com
REQUIREMENTS Windows XP/Vista
FILE SIZE 2MB

This wizard-based tool provides a simple way of improving the colour balance, brightness and contrast of your digital snaps. Load one or more photos into Alamoon Color Enhancer, select the options you want – these range from Auto Levels and Auto Tone to Gamma Correction and Colorize – and the software will do the rest. You can also convert one image file format to another, resize pictures and add a watermark.

SERIF PANORAMAPLUS
http://bit.ly/serif259
REQUIREMENTS Windows XP/Vista/7
FILE SIZE 24.3MB

The latest version of PanoramaPlus costs £14 to buy but you can bag a free Starter Edition from Serif's Free Downloads site. You create horizontal and vertical panoramas from your pictures simply by importing a set of photos and then clicking Stitch. PanoramaPlus seamlessly stitches together multiple shots and lets you fine-tune the result using its straighten and crop tools. Panoramas can be saved in various image formats and shared on Facebook and Flickr.

PHOTO TIPS

PHOTO3X2

www.mmsoft.pl

REQUIREMENTS Windows XP/Vista/7

FILE SIZE 382KB

If all you want to do is crop a photo or change its aspect ratio without resizing or stretching the image, this is the ideal tool for the job. Photo3x2 loads instantly and is very easy to use. Just drag and drop a photo onto the interface, then select a pre-set or custom option. You can also rotate a photo in 90-degree steps or flip the image horizontally.

TSR WATERMARK IMAGE

www.watermark-image.com

REQUIREMENTS Windows XP/Vista/7

FILE SIZE 464KB

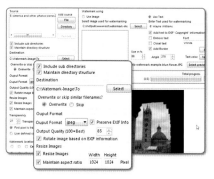

Watermarking photos helps you prevent anyone stealing them or claiming credit for your work. This program lets you add text or graphics to a single image or a whole batch of photos at once. You can adjust the transparency and choose the size and location of the watermark. The program also lets you embed messages in a photo's EXIF data, and everything is handled through one simple screen.

DROPRESIZE

www.dropresize.com

REQUIREMENTS Windows XP/Vista/7

FILE SIZE 74.9KB

If you regularly resize images to the same dimensions, this simple application can save you a lot of time and effort.

Once you've set your preferences, Dropresize will sit in your System Tray and monitor a folder of your choosing. You simply drag and drop new images into this folder and the program will automatically resize them for you.

UNSHAKE

http://bit.ly/unshake259

REQUIREMENTS Windows XP/Vista/7, Mac OS X

FILE SIZE 1MB

Modern digital cameras have all sorts of clever features designed to help you take the best possible photos. Sometimes, however, they still produce shaky or out-of-focus shots. Although Unshake can't completely correct a blurred image, it usually manages to improve the quality of the photo. You can switch between normal and severe blur and select one of the preset options, or have the program guess the correct settings. There are various other options to play around with, too.

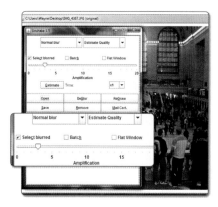

PHOTO MAGICIAN

http://sheldonsolutions.co.uk/photomagician

REQUIREMENTS Windows XP/Vista/7

FILE SIZE 1.6MB

Photo Magician is a speedy batch-resizing/conversion tool. Choose your input and output folders, pick a preset profile or manually choose the size to scale images to. You can opt to scan sub-folders, overwrite the originals and turn the image preview function on or off.

There's also a Quick Convert Mode that displays a magician's hat icon. Drop some images into this and they'll be automatically converted using your preset preferences.

SMILLAENLARGER

http://imageenlarger.sourceforge.net

REQUIREMENTS Windows XP/Vista/7

FILE SIZE 6.6MB

Usually when you increase the size of a small photo, it loses detail and can become corrupt or pixellated. This program uses its own algorithms to solve that problem and can generate much higher-quality images. Load a photo and pick the desired size, then play around with the parameter sliders until the preview looks right. Finally, click Calculate to resize the photo.

INSTANTMASK

http://clipping-path-studio.com/instantmask

REQUIREMENTS Windows XP/Vista/7

FILE SIZE 5.3MB

Cutting out a person or object or removing the background from a photograph can be one of the trickiest and most time-consuming photo-editing tasks. InstantMask offers a quick and simple method that produces decent results. To use the program, select the green (keep) marker and draw around the inside of the item that you want (this doesn't need to be done particularly neatly). Then select the red (remove) maker and draw around the outside of the object. Click Preview to see the cutout and, if you're happy with how it looks, click the Save button to export the image to your hard disk.

FOTO-MOSAIK-EDDA

www.sixdots.de/mosaik/en

REQUIREMENTS Windows XP/Vista/7

FILE SIZE 2.2MB

This program lets you create impressive photo mosaics made up of lots and lots of much smaller pictures (tiles). Start by pointing the software in the direction of your image library. The more photos this contains, the better the end results will be. When all the pictures have been added to Foto-Mosaik-Edda's database (this can take a while), you'll need to select a photo to turn into a mosaic. You can choose how complicated you want the result to be, and specify how many times a single source tile can be used.

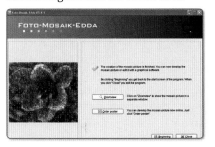

FOTOMORPH

www.diphso.no/FotoMorph.html

REQUIREMENTS Windows XP/Vista/7

FILE SIZE 6.2MB

Morphing one photo into another can produce some fun results. FotoMorph lets you create your own morphs, warps, pans and photo transitions. Choose a type of project and load some images. Add your control points – these tell the program where corresponding spots are on each photograph. For example, if you're morphing a photo of a man into a dog, you could start by adding a control point to the man's left eye. FotoMorph will then add a point to the dog picture, which you drag to the dog's left eye, to indicate where the photo of the dog

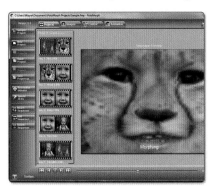

corresponds to the photo of the man. The more control points you add, the better the results will be. You can also add text and a background.

COLLAGEIT

www.collageitfree.com

REQUIREMENTS Windows XP/Vista/7, Mac OS X

FILE SIZE 4.9MB

Use your digital snaps to create collages by selecting some images and picking a background. You can control the spacing, margin and rotation of each image, and shuffle the pictures around until you get an arrangement you like. Click the plus sign in the corner to view the collage full size. Layouts can be saved for future use.

PHOTO TITLE

www.phototitle.com

REQUIREMENTS Windows XP/Vista/7

FILE SIZE 2MB

This tool lets you add text, time stamps (pulled from the EXIF data), speech bubbles and pictures to your photographs. Simply load an image into Photo Title and choose what you want to add. You can adjust the photo's saturation, brightness and contrast, and rotate and resize it.

The software can also batch-process a collection of images – useful if you want

to add a date and time watermark to all the pictures in a folder, for example.

FRAMEFUN

http://bit.ly/framefun

REQUIREMENTS Windows XP/Vista/7

FILE SIZE 1.2MB

As you'd expect with a name like FrameFun, this program lets you add fun and interesting frames, borders and shadows to your photos. You can apply the additions to a single image, or to a whole load of pictures in one go. There are a reasonable number of options to play around with, and you can achieve some appealing results with a little trial and error.

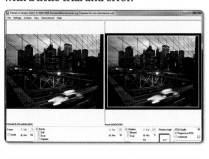

PHOTO-BONNY

www.photo-bon.com/en

REQUIREMENTS Windows XP/Vista

FILE SIZE 23.5MB

With Photo-Bonny you can liven up your photographs by adding some fun clip art, shapes and frames to them. Just drag the items you want to your picture, and resize and rotate them accordingly. Objects are added as layers, so they can easily be manipulated further or deleted.

Photo-Bonny also lets you draw on your photos with coloured pencils and use the eraser tool to rub out any mistakes. The photo viewer displays information about an image, and lets you rate it and add comments.

Recover lost photos for free

If you've accidentally deleted valuable images from your PC or camera, don't despair. Here are seven free ways to get your precious pictures back

Most of us have experienced that heart-stopping moment when we realise we've accidentally deleted an important file. Erasing a personal photo can be particularly traumatic because pictures often have sentimental value and – unlike music or software – you can't simply download them again. Similarly, a corrupt memory card in your camera may mean a whole holiday's snaps are lost forever. Thankfully, there are a number of steps you can take to recover lost photos.

CHECK YOUR RECYCLE BIN

It sounds obvious, but before you start panicking over missing photos, it's worth

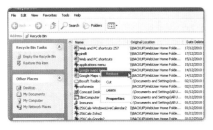

looking in the Recycle Bin. If you haven't emptied it for a while, click the Date Deleted column to reorganise its contents with the most recently deleted items at the top. To rescue a picture from the Bin, right-click the file and select Restore. If you can't see your deleted photo, try showing hidden files by going to Tools, Folder Options, View and selecting 'Show hidden files, folders and drives'.

SEARCH YOUR HARD DISK

There's a chance that the photo may have been moved to a different folder rather than deleted from your PC. Try running the Windows search tool for 'Pictures and Photos' or use a Desktop search program such as Google Desktop (http://desktop.google.com). Obviously, the more you can remember of the file name the better, but you can always sort results by date modified and try searching by file extension, such as '*.jpg', to make things easier. Generally,

you should only need to search your My Documents folder and perhaps your Desktop (if it's messy!).

RUN THE RECUVA WIZARD

Recuva (www.piriform.com/recuva), which is from the same software stable as CCleaner, is an essential tool to have on your PC. This powerful free data-recovery program offers a dedicated 'wizard' for rescuing lost images, which makes the entire process pleasantly painless. It also has a Deep Scan mode for more comprehensive image scouring. You can retrieve files that have been

ESSENTIAL RECOVERY TIPS

■ If you want to rescue lost photos, don't take any more! Any pictures that you save to your camera's memory card could overwrite your lost images, reducing your chance of getting them back.
■ Save your restored photos to a different drive on your PC or, if possible, to a USB memory stick. This will prevent you from overwriting any other images you want to save.
■ Keep a 'recovery toolkit' of programs such as Recuva and Zero

Assumption Recovery (see above) stored on a USB drive so they're ready to run if you ever accidentally delete a photo.
■ If your memory card has a write-protect switch, flick it to 'on' so that the data on it can't be overwritten.
■ If nothing works, try a data-recovery company such as Kroll Ontrack (www.ontrackdatarecovery.co.uk). Prices vary according to the type of data loss, but you can request a quote online.

deleted from your camera's memory card, your PC's My Documents folder, Recycle Bin and other locations, and restore them to the destination of your choice.

There's also a portable version of Recuva (http://bit.ly/recuva258). This requires no installation so it won't overwrite any precious data when you run it. See our Mini Workshop (right) to find out how to use Recuva.

TRY PC INSPECTOR SMART RECOVERY

If Recuva can't find your lost photos, try PC Inspector Smart Recovery 4.5 (http://bit.ly/pcinspector258). This excellent free program will restore deleted and corrupted images from most memory cards, as well as your hard disk and USB drive. The software supports a wide range of image and movie file formats, and handily displays thumbnails of JPEGs in its search results to help you quickly identify the pictures you're after. Like Recuva, PC Inspector Smart Recovery offers both a fast-scanning mode and a deeper, much slower Intensive mode and will restore pictures to the destination of your choice.

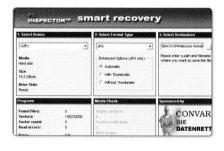

GIVE ZERO ASSUMPTION RECOVERY A GO

Zero Assumption Recovery, or ZAR, (www.z-a-recovery.com) is another useful tool for rescuing deleted images. The program is particularly good at retrieving photos from corrupt and accidentally formatted memory cards, and supports a wide range of image

formats. The software lets you preview each picture before you restore it, to save you rescuing unwanted files. Recovering images using ZAR is completely free, but the program does include some other features that require registration.

RESCUE PHOTOS FROM A DAMAGED DISC

Storing your pictures on a CD or DVD is a great way to archive them, but if the disc gets damaged, you're in trouble. Help is at hand from the free CD Recovery Toolbox (http://bit.ly/cdrec258). It's designed for retrieving unreadable files from damaged CDs and DVDs. Once you've installed the program, simply select the drive you want to restore from, choose the files you want to rescue and click Save.

CHECK ONLINE ACCOUNTS FOR BACKUPS

If you've uploaded pictures to Facebook (www.facebook.com), Flickr (www.flickr.com) or photo-printing services such as PhotoBox (www.photobox.co.uk), you've effectively created backup copies in the process. If you've accidentally deleted an old photo from your hard disk or camera, it's worth checking your online accounts to see if you've previously uploaded it. You might not be able to download it at the original resolution, but at least you'll have a version of the image.

MINI WORKSHOP

Retrieve lost photos using Recuva

1 When you first run Recuva, the recovery wizard should start automatically. If not, it means the program has started in Advanced mode. Launch Recuva by clicking the Options button ❶ and then clicking the Run Wizard button on the General tab ❷. You can also choose to 'Show Wizard at startup' ❸.

2 Select the Pictures option, then specify where the photos were deleted from, such as a memory card ❶ or the Recycle Bin ❷. If you don't know, choose 'I'm not sure' ❸. Click Next, then Start. Recuva will scan for and display all retrievable image files. Select the ones you want and click the Recover button.

3 If your initial search doesn't turn up the photos you're looking for, click the 'Switch to advanced mode' button, then click Options, Actions and Deep Scan ❶. Click OK, and Recuva will search for your images more thoroughly and colour-code the results according to their quality ❷.

PHOTO TIPS

BACKUP & STORAGE

p78

BACKUP & STORAGE

How to
BACK UP YOUR PC LOCALLY FOR FREE

Find out how to keep your files and folders safe with the minimum of hassle

You never know when computer disaster will strike. Corrupted files, crashes and hard-disk failure can all lead to a permanent loss of data. Fortunately, backing up any irreplaceable personal content so you're prepared for the worst is surprisingly straightforward. Windows comes with its own tool for the job, but we recommend you go for a third-party program instead, as they offer more options and flexibility.

When backing up your computer, don't forget about important but often overlooked essentials such as bookmarks, emails, drivers and even saved games.

MAKE A LIST OF YOUR INSTALLED SOFTWARE

If your hard disk were to die tomorrow, would you be able to name every single program you had installed on it? Probably not. For that reason it's worth making a note of all the applications on your computer and checking you have the installation discs or downloaded files stored somewhere safe.

Although you can do this manually, it's much easier to use Belarc Advisor

www.belarc.com/free_download.html). Simply install the software and wait while the program creates a profile of your computer. When it's finished, the results will load in a new browser window and you can scroll down to the software section to see the full list.

What's particularly helpful is that the program will also show you the licence keys for all your installed Microsoft

Belarc Advisor makes a list of your installed applications so you can store the program discs and downloaded files somewhere safe

Before you archive your emails with MailStore Home, get rid of any messages you don't need

products, so reinstallation will be easy. You can print the page or save it to disk.

BACK UP YOUR EMAILS

MailStore Home (www.mailstore.com) works with all popular email clients, including Outlook, Thunderbird and Windows Mail. It can even back up your webmail. Just click the Archive E-mail option and select a message source.

You can choose which folders you want to back up – some, such as drafts, junk and deleted files, will be automatically excluded – and configure any other settings. The archiving process can take a while to complete depending on the size of your inbox. For this reason, it's worth clearing out any unwanted emails such as newsletters before you begin. The software will automatically reduce the

Picasa makes short work of finding, organising and backing up your photographs

Firefox's built-in synchronisation makes your browser information accessible on any PC

space your emails take up by saving only the first instance of an attachment.

....

COPY YOUR IMAGES

Backing up your photos is just a case of copying them from one disk to another, or writing the files to CD or DVD. Picasa (http://picasa.google.com) can locate images scattered across several hard disks and simplify the process of backing them up. Just go to Tools, Back Up Pictures and create or edit a set. Click Select All (you'll want to check for duplicates and make sure it hasn't selected anything you don't require), then click Burn. Picasa will tell you how many CDs or DVDs you'll need to back up your entire photo library.

....

BACK UP YOUR BROWSER

There's more to your browser than just bookmarks. It can store browsing history, passwords, form details,

preferences and more. Google Chrome and Firefox 4 both have a built-in Sync feature to save your data and make it accessible from anywhere.

You can also back up your information using a program such as FavBackup (www.favbrowser.com/backup). This doesn't require installation and works with all the major browsers. Just select the ones you use, then choose the data to save and a location to save it to.

....

BACK UP YOUR DRIVERS

It's probably not something you'd give much thought to, but backing up device drivers can save you a lot of problems and messing around trying to find obscure ones later on. SlimDrivers (www.slimdrivers.com) can search your computer and copy all the currently installed drivers to a new location. Click the Backup button and choose what you want to include. Click on Backup To and browse to the folder you want to use.

MINI WORKSHOP

Back up your computer with Comodo Backup

1 Comodo Backup (http://backup.comodo.com) is very easy to use. Install it and restart your PC, then click the Backup option **1** and choose the type you want **2**. Select the source folders and files **3** – 'Disk, Partitions and MBR' is the most comprehensive option, but you can also back up files and folders, the Registry, emails and more.

....

2 Next, choose a destination. Select My Computer **1** and you can pick a folder or another disk. You can also write the data to disc or copy it to a networked location. Click the alarm clock icon **2** to schedule a backup or Backup Now **3** to begin writing the files. Click Next **4** for more options.

....

3 Advanced mode lets you change the archive settings, including the compression level, and choose certain file types to exclude, such as .tmp and .bak files. The program can be set to email you when a scheduled task has completed or failed **1**. To load a previous back-up, click Restore **2** and follow the instructions.

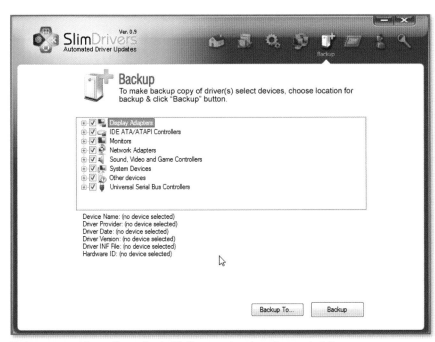

Backing up your drivers will prove invaluable if you ever have to perform a reinstall

How to
BACK UP YOUR DATA ONLINE

Using an internet service to store your files and documents means they'll be safe and accessible from anywhere. Here we take you through the options

S aving a copy of your personal data on the internet means you'll always have access to it and can download important files from anywhere. There are plenty of free services on offer, although these often come with restrictions, such as a limited allocation of storage space and a cap on the number of files you can upload or download at a time. If you want to back up a lot of content and be certain that it's being stored safely and securely, then a paid-for plan might suit you better.

BACK UP VIA EMAIL

One of the simplest ways to back up smaller files is to use a service called BackupElf (http://backupelf.com). There's no download required – you simply compose a new email message, attach your files and send it to save@backupelf. com. The service then securely stores messages and attachments.

The free version gives you up to 100MB of storage. If you need more, you can upgrade to one of the paid options:

Basic, which provides 1GB of storage for $4.95 a month (around £3); Popular, which provides 5GB for $9.95 a month (around £6); or Premium, which provides 10GB for $19.95 a month (around £12).

USE A GMAIL ACCOUNT FOR STORAGE

Sign up for a Gmail account and you get over 7GB of free space that can be used to back up your files. You can simply email the data to yourself, or use the GMail Drive Shell Extension (www. viksoe.dk/code/gmail.htm), which will transform your account into a virtual hard disk that appears in Windows Explorer and is accessible from your computer's Desktop.

To set it up, run the installer, click the GMail Drive entry in Windows Explorer

Small files can be emailed to BackupElf as attachments and stored on the site

The GMail Drive Shell Extension turns your Gmail account into a virtual hard disk

and enter the username and password of the Gmail account you wish to use. Tick Auto Login if you want the application to remember your details. You can drag and drop files to and from the virtual drive just like any other storage space and delete any unwanted files.

Store your photos online and you'll never risk losing all those precious memories

Paid-for storage such as Carbonite is convenient, safe and very reasonably priced

USE ADRIVE

Sign up to ADrive (www.adrive.com) and you'll get a whopping 50GB of free storage for your data. You can upload, download and share files, and edit documents in Zoho (www.zoho.com).

Certain features, such as FTP support and the Desktop tool, are available only if you register for a paid account. You can try the premium features for free by signing up for a 14-day trial.

BACK UP PHOTOS AND VIDEOS

Your hard disk is probably home to thousands of digital photos – treasured memories that would be impossible to replace. You can back these up online by uploading them to sites such as Flickr (www.flickr.com), Picasa Web Albums (http://picasaweb.google.com) and Facebook (www.facebook.com). If you're thinking of getting prints and photo gifts, you can also use PhotoBox (www. photobox.co.uk) to store your images.

Videos can be uploaded to YouTube (www.youtube.com) and downloaded again when required in MP4 format. You'll find the Download MP4 option in the drop-down menu under the clip on your videos page.

....

PAID-FOR OPTIONS

Free online backup services are great, but if you need more space it's worth paying for a decent storage solution. Carbonite (www.carbonite.co.uk) gives you unlimited capacity for a very reasonable £41.95 a year. You can upload and download as much data as you like and your files will be automatically backed up every time you make a change. There's a 15-day free trial available.

Another excellent service is Mozy (http://mozy.co.uk). Its simple Home online backup service costs £4.99 a month. If you want to try it out without spending any money, a free 2GB version is also available.

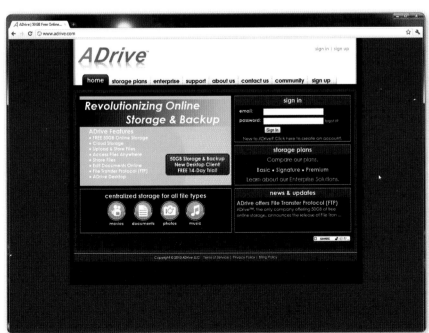

ADrive offers a very generous 50GB of free storage to house your files and media

MINI WORKSHOP

Back up your files to SkyDrive

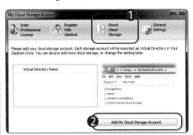

1 Microsoft's online storage site (http://skydrive.live.com) gives you up to 25GB of space for free. You can upload files via your web browser, but Gladinet Cloud Desktop (free from www.gladinet.com) makes it even easier. Install it, click Mount Cloud Storage ❶ and click Add My Cloud Storage Account ❷.

2 In the Storage Provider drop-down box, select Windows Live SkyDrive. Click Next and enter your Windows Live ID and password ❶. Click Next again and agree to the terms and conditions. The program will install as a virtual drive. If you have more than one SkyDrive account, just repeat the process.

3 Your virtual storage space will be assigned a drive letter ❶. This is Z: by default, but you can change it ❷ and the drive label. You can also change the cache location ❸ and turn on profile encryption if required ❹. Back up files by dragging them to the virtual drive in Windows Explorer.

How to
BACK UP YOUR GADGETS

Losing all the data on your phone could be almost as disastrous as losing the files on your PC. Fortunately, backing up your mobile devices needn't cost a fortune

Today's mobile phones are capable of a lot more than simply making and receiving calls. They can take photographs and record video, store notes and emails, keep you in touch with your social networks and manage a busy schedule. If your phone were to go missing, you'd lose a lot of personal data, much of it probably irreplaceable. Fortunately, it's very easy to back up your phone and other portable devices, so you'll at least be prepared should disaster strike.

BACK UP YOUR IPHONE USING ITUNES

When you sync or perform an update on your iPhone, iPod Touch or iPad, iTunes will automatically back it up. You can manually force a backup or restore whenever you like by right-clicking (or Ctrl + clicking) the device's entry in iTunes and selecting the relevant option. You can store only one backup for each connected device at a time with iTunes, but it's easy to copy a backup if you want to keep more than one.

Navigate to Users\[username]\AppData\Roaming\Apple Computer\MobileSync\Backup in Windows 7 or Vista, or to Documents and Settings\[username]\Application Data\Apple Computer\MobileSync\Backup in XP. Mac OS X users will find their backups stored in the

Library/Application Support/MobileSync/Backup folder.

The backup will contain your address book, calendar information, call history, photos, videos, passwords, mail accounts, notes, bookmarks, history, text messages, voice memos and wallpapers. It will also save your App Store application settings, preferences, data and in-app purchases, although it won't back up the applications themselves.

....

KEEP GOOGLE SERVICES IN SYNC

Google Sync (www.google.com/mobile/sync) ensures that you always have the latest Gmail, Calendar and Contacts data available on your phone by backing up your data online. It's a two-way service, so when you add, delete or change

iTunes will automatically back up your iPhone when it performs an update

something on your mobile, the same details will be updated online and on all your other connected devices.

If you lose your phone or it gets damaged, you can simply connect your replacement model and all your important information will be restored. The software works with most leading smartphones, including BlackBerry, iPhone and Windows Mobile models.

Google Sync keeps all your Gmail, Calendar and Contacts details updated

Back up the music from your iPod or iPhone with the free SharePod app

COPY MUSIC FROM AN IPOD

SharePod (www.getsharepod.com) lets you copy songs directly to your computer from any iPod or iPhone. The software doesn't require any installation – you simply run it and connect your device. Your plugged-in iPod or iPhone should be detected automatically and you'll be able to browse and copy the files you want to it.

SEND YOUR MOBILE SNAPS TO FLICKR

You can email photos from your phone directly to Flickr using your unique upload address. To find this, go to http://m.flickr.com on your mobile and sign in. Click the More tab and select Upload. You will now see your upload address displayed. The subject line is used as the title of your photo and the body text as the description.

You can add tags at the same time. Flickr also lets you use certain address variations to specify who has access to

your uploaded photos: everyone, friends, family, friends and family, or just you.

If you prefer something more advanced, there are Flickr apps available for the iPhone, BlackBerry, Android and other mobile devices. Go to the Yahoo Mobile page at http://mobile.yahoo.com/flickr for more information.

BACK UP YOUR MEMORY CARD

Many modern mobile phones make use of Micro SD cards to store data. These are about the size of a fingernail and come in various capacities. You can move your contacts and photos to the card, then copy them on to your computer.

You'll need a memory card reader and possibly a Micro SD-to-SD card adaptor to do this, but these are generally very cheap. MyMemory (www.mymemory.co.uk) has one for just £1.99 (http://bit.ly/howto1255).

You can upload photos from your smartphone direct to Flickr so they'll be accessible from anywhere

MINI WORKSHOP

Back up contacts with Syncfriend

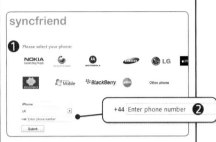

1 Go to www.syncfriend.com and either create a new account or log in with your existing details for Google, Windows Live, Yahoo, Facebook or Flickr. You'll be prompted to select your phone. Click on the manufacturer's name ❶ and choose the model, country and operator, then enter your phone number ❷.

2 On the welcome screen you'll find details on how to set up your phone ❶. This process varies depending on the model. Android, BlackBerry, iPhone and Windows Mobile users will need to install a free or trial version first.

3 Sync your device. When done, click the Phonebook tab ❶ to view your contacts ❷. Select an entry to edit the information ❸ or remove it ❹. Invite a friend to use the service ❺ and you can update each other's private contact details. If you've synced your schedule, access it through the Calendar tab ❻.

Best sites for
FREE ONLINE STORAGE

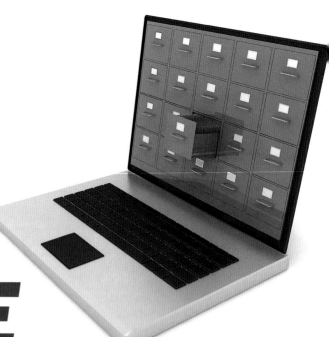

Online storage services give you access to your files and folders from any web-connected computer. We test six of the best free options

Dropbox
★★★★★
www.dropbox.com

EASE OF USE ★★★★★ **FEATURES** ★★★★☆ **PERFORMANCE** ★★★★★ **STORAGE SPACE** ★★★★☆

WHAT WE LIKE

When Dropbox launched in 2008, it became the file-sharing option of choice for many web users. And once you start using this excellent service, you'll probably wonder how you managed to survive without it.

The main benefits of the Dropbox offering are its focus and simplicity. While other online storage services we've reviewed here pile complexity into their synchronisation options, Dropbox's proposition is a single folder that's synchronised across all computers associated with the same Dropbox account.

This means you can simply install the software, then throw some files and folders into the My Dropbox folder to upload them to the Dropbox server. Open the My Dropbox folder on a second PC, and the files appear as soon as they've downloaded. You can also access the content via your web browser.

Any number of devices can be associated with a Dropbox

account – including most modern smartphones – and 2GB of storage space is included with free accounts. Add in file-versioning (where older versions of files are accessible via the web interface) and some basic file-sharing facilities and you'll find Dropbox hard to beat.

HOW IT CAN BE IMPROVED

Mac users might find it quite tricky to upgrade to new versions of Dropbox, and

we'd like to see this process made easier. Keep an eye out for improvements in beta versions of Dropbox, which are available from the forums (http://forums.dropbox.com). You can also request new features here.

OUR VERDICT

Dropbox wins hands-down for its wonderful simplicity and reliability. The interface couldn't be easier to use, and the service works with a minimum of fuss.

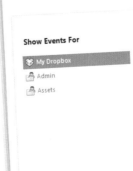

IDrive Basic

★★★★☆

www.idrive.com

EASE OF USE ★★★★☆   **FEATURES** ★★★☆☆   **PERFORMANCE** ★★★☆☆
STORAGE SPACE ★★★★☆

WHAT WE LIKE

To get the most out of IDrive, you need two distinct tools: IDrive Classic and IDrive Explorer. Classic is a backup component that you use to upload files to the site. Explorer is optional but is actually the better tool, as it turns the free 2GB of online storage space that IDrive gives you into a virtual drive and lets you access content through Windows Explorer. However, IDrive Explorer can only be used for restoring files, so you need to use IDrive Classic to put files on the site in the first place.

By selecting the Continuous Backup mode in IDrive Classic, you can keep data synchronised to IDrive's servers. Backed-up files can also be accessed from the IDrive web interface, so you can get at them from anywhere. Sadly, there are no options for sharing your files with other people.

HOW IT CAN BE IMPROVED

Rather than maintaining two separate tools for the same service, IDrive would be simpler to use if they were combined. It would also be good to be able to drag and drop files to and from the IDrive Explorer virtual drive.

OUR VERDICT

IDrive Classic works well as a backup tool and IDrive Explorer makes for easy restoration, but the service would be better accessed via a unified interface.

Box Lite

★★★★☆

http://box.net

EASE OF USE ★★★☆☆   **FEATURES** ★★★★☆   **PERFORMANCE** ★★★★☆
STORAGE SPACE ★★★★☆

WHAT WE LIKE

Box tries harder than any other service here to hold your hand through its service, explaining how to create a folder and upload files. This is a good thing, as Box's interface is rather muddled.

Free Lite accounts offer an impressive 5GB of storage, but the upload cap of 25MB per file is very restrictive. The Business plan, which costs $15 (around £9) per month, increases these limits to 500GB and 2GB respectively.

Box's best feature is its drag-and-drop uploader. It isn't perfect – we struggled to get it to work properly in Internet Explorer – but it copes with individual files and whole folders, unlike Microsoft's SkyDrive (right), which can't handle folders.

Box also offers some quick and simple sharing features,

such as password-protected links for specific files and folders.

HOW IT CAN BE IMPROVED

The 25MB file limit has to go for starters, and the interface needs a thorough overhaul. The over-enthusiastic use of pop-up tips is also off-putting.

OUR VERDICT

Box is great to try if you want to share files as well as store them online. It's better than Dropbox in this respect, but otherwise it's too fiddly for our liking.

BEST OF THE REST

Windows Live SkyDrive

www.windowslive.co.uk/skydrive.aspx

Like many other Microsoft products these days, Windows Live SkyDrive is a bit of a mess. There's 25GB of free storage, but restrictions on how you can use it and no desktop integration. Add to this a 50MB file-size limit and there's little incentive to try the service.

The one upside is that SkyDrive integrates directly with Office Web Apps, the online version of Microsoft Office.

ADrive Basic

www.adrive.com

ADrive doesn't scrimp on free storage space – there's 50GB on offer just for signing up. However, the service is clunky to use, with an interface that resembles the XP-era Windows Explorer, but operates more slowly.

You might want to exploit ADrive as a free way to back up a sizeable chunk of files every now and then but using it on a day-to-day basis would quickly drive you to distraction.

Metahyper

www.metahyper.com

Metahyper is most suitable for short-term file-sharing, rather than long-term online storage. Sign up for a free account and you'll get 20GB of storage and the ability to upload files of up to 1GB in size.

However, even Metahyper's paid-for premium accounts have built-in expiry dates on uploaded files, ranging from 15 to 545 days – and worryingly, it's unclear whether or when files residing in free accounts may expire.

SPRING-CLEAN YOUR PC

p88

SPRING-CLEAN YOUR PC FOR FREE

A thorough clear-out can give even the most sluggish of systems a new lease of life. Here we present 30 advanced tips to help you speed up your PC's performance – and they won't cost you a penny

I f your PC takes forever to boot and every function it performs seems to take an age, you don't have to sit there cursing your luck and twiddling your thumbs: you can do something about it. Uninstalling programs you no longer use, clearing out junk files and clutter, defragging your hard disk and optimising the Registry will all make a huge difference to your system's performance.

Many of the tools you need come as part of your Windows operating system, but there are other free programs that do an even better job. Devote a little time to a spring-clean and you'll be well rewarded – your PC will be faster, more responsive and less prone to crashing.

Over the next few pages, we show you 30 ways to clear out virtual rubbish, polish up your PC and fix hidden problems.

SPRING-CLEAN YOUR PC

COMPLETELY REMOVE UNWANTED PROGRAMS

Start your spring-clean by uninstalling any software that you don't use on a regular basis. Instead of using Windows' own rather clunky tool, we'd recommend a third-party solution such as IObit Uninstaller (www.iobit.com/advanceduninstaller.html).

This free program lets you uninstall several applications at once, and it can forcibly remove any stubborn software. IObit Uninstaller can also clear out items left behind by the standard uninstall process, including user data and Registry entries.

Additionally, if you've unwittingly installed multiple browser toolbars, the software can remove them for you.

CLEAR UP AFTER ANTI-VIRUS SOFTWARE

Most anti-virus programs are easily removed, but some leave behind files and Registry entries that can interfere with the smooth running of your replacement security software.

AppRemover (www.appremover.com) is designed to uninstall any unwanted security products thoroughly and clean up after failed removal attempts. The program recognises and works with all popular anti-virus programs, including Norton (www.symantec.com), McAfee (www.mcafee.com/uk) and AVG (http://free.avg.com).

RUN POPULAR PROGRAMS FROM THE CLOUD

It's a rather radical idea, but instead of filling your hard disk with downloaded programs, you can use the new Spoon plug-in (http://spoon.net) to run them directly from the web as and when required. You simply sign up for an account on the website, browse the Spoon database to find the program you want and hit Launch to run it.

The selection of software on offer is already impressive – Skype, Foxit Reader, OpenOffice.org and VLC Media Player, to name just a few – and new apps are being added all the time.

Virtualised programs take a little longer to launch from the cloud, but once up and running they're exactly the same as those installed on your hard disk.

CLEAR AWAY THE LEFTOVERS FROM PROGRAMS

BleachBit (http://bleachbit.sourceforge.net) is a useful new system-cleaning tool that can find and remove temporary files, old backups, thumbnail caches, DNS pre-fetch data and auto-fill history, as well as clean up after your browser and other applications. The free program can even remove uninstallers for Microsoft updates, including those for hotfixes and service packs.

BleachBit can also shred files and overwrite free disk space to prevent the recovery of any previously deleted data. To find out how to use the program, see our Mini Workshop on page 84.

LOCATE AND REMOVE DISK-SPACE HOGS

TreeSize Free (www.jam-software.com/treesize_free) analyses your hard disk and shows you at a glance where all your free space has gone.

Choose a drive or directory to scan and the program will show you the size of each folder, subfolder and file (in KB, MB or GB) and let you open, run, rename or delete an item. You can sort the folders by name or size.

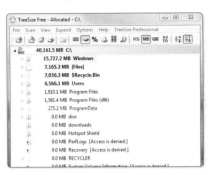

FIND AND REMOVE DUPLICATE FILES

It can be surprisingly easy to accumulate duplicate copies of a file, especially photos. These serve no purpose other than to waste your disk space, so it's worth using the latest version of Duplicate Cleaner (www.digitalvolcano.co.uk) to locate them.

Just set the criteria, click Scan Now and this fast, free tool will find and let you delete duplicate files.

CLEAR OUT THE PROGRAM FILES FOLDER

When you uninstall a program, all traces of it should be eradicated, but that's often not the case. Navigate to the Program Files folder (C:\Program Files or C:\Program Files (x86) in Windows 7) and you may come across empty sub-folders for software that you long ago removed from your system.

To get rid of these folders, simply select them and press Delete. Make sure you've uninstalled the programs in question before you remove their folders.

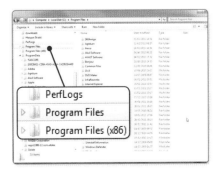

Scrub your system using BleachBit

1 Once you've installed BleachBit (http://bleachbit.sourceforge.net), launch the software and select the name of a program in the left-hand column ❶. Choose the elements you want to delete by ticking the individual tick boxes ❷ – a description of each entry is displayed in the area on the right ❸.

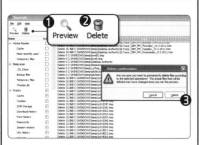

2 To view the items you're removing and find out how much disk space you'll save, click the Preview button in the top-left corner ❶. Choose any other program entries you want to erase and then click the Delete icon ❷. When the confirmation box appears, click Delete again ❸.

3 As well as deleting files, BleachBit can also 'shred' – or overwrite – them so they can't be recovered. To do this, click the File menu and choose Shred Files ❶. Select the file you want to shred and click Open ❷. When the Delete Confirmation box appears, click Delete.

MAKE CCLEANER MORE POWERFUL

CCleaner (www.piriform.com/ccleaner) does a great job of removing leftover and temporary junk files from your hard disk. CCEnhancer (http://bit.ly/ccenhancer) is a small tool that adds support for hundreds of additional applications, making the cleaning program even more useful. The new entries are integrated seamlessly into CCleaner and marked with an asterisk so you can see what the program has found.

DELETE OLD DATA FROM FIREFOX AND CHROME

Your browser caches a lot of data, so it's definitely worth giving it a good clear out on a regular basis. Click&Clean (www.hotcleaner.com) is available as an add-on for Firefox and Chrome, and there's also a Desktop version. It can erase your browsing and download history, remove temporary files and cookies, clear typed URLs and delete saved data you've typed into online forums.

The Chrome version also includes the ability to scan your system for malware using BitDefender QuickScan.

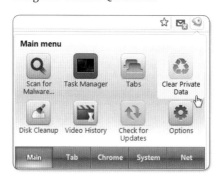

REDUCE THE SIZE OF YOUR RECYCLE BIN

By default, the Windows Recycle Bin uses up a fair amount of disk space. However, you can reduce this by right-clicking the bin icon, selecting Properties and choosing a new size. If you have multiple hard disks, you'll need to apply

your change to each of them. Older files that no longer fit in the smaller bin will be deleted automatically.

REMOVE UNWANTED WINDOWS 7 FEATURES

Microsoft's latest operating system comes with a lot of tools and functions that you'll probably never use or require, and disabling these unwanted features can speed up your PC.

To do this, go to Start, Control Panel, Programs and click the 'Turn Windows features on or off' link. Clear a feature's tick box to disable it – you can always turn it on again if you change your mind.

TURN OFF WINDOWS DEFENDER

Windows Defender is built into Windows 7 and protects your system from spyware and other potentially harmful software. If you're already running a good anti-spyware program, however, you can safely disable Defender

to free up resources. To do this, click Start and type Defender into the box that appears. Open Windows Defender and click Tools, then Options. Click the Administrator link on the left and untick 'Use this program'.

REMOVE OLD SYSTEM RESTORE POINTS

Windows automatically creates restore points whenever you install a program or new hardware device. While these can prove a lifesaver if a program or a piece of hardware messes up your PC, they take up a fair bit of space.

To remove all but the most recent restore point, right-click the C: drive in Computer, and select Properties. Click the Disk Cleanup button under the General tab and wait for the tool to calculate how much space can be recovered. Select 'Clean up system files', then click the More Options tab, and finally click 'Clean up' under System Restore.

ADJUST SYSTEM RESTORE'S DISK USAGE

You can manually alter how much space Windows 7 devotes to the System Restore feature. Go to Start, right-click Computer and select Properties, and then click the System Protection link on the left-hand side.

The System Properties box will open at the System Protection tab. Select the drive you want and click Configure.

Drag the slider to change the amount of space available for restore points.

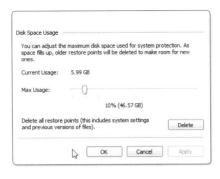

COMPRESS YOUR EMAILS

Switching to a webmail service such as Gmail (http://mail.google.com) is the easiest way to avoid cluttering your hard disk with old messages. If you prefer to have desktop access to your emails, use the free archiving tool MailStore Home (www.mailstore.com) to create a compressed backup of your messages. It works with all major email applications, including Thunderbird, Outlook and Outlook Express/Windows Live Mail, and can even archive messages directly to CD.

BACK UP YOUR FILES ONLINE FOR FREE

Because you never know when disaster will strike, it's vital to back up your important data regularly. Storing files 'in the cloud', or online will let you access them from anywhere. There are plenty of excellent free and paid-for storage services available.

If you only want to back up (and optionally share) your most important files, you should consider getting a Dropbox account (www.dropbox.com). This initially gives 2GB of free storage, but you can increase this by doing things such as referring friends.

SkyDrive, Microsoft's online storage site (http://skydrive.live.com), offers 25GB for free and has a 50MB per file limit, making it ideal for storing smaller items such as photos and documents. ADrive (www.adrive.com) gives you a generous 50GB of free online storage, although certain features, such as the desktop client and FTP support, are available only to premium users.

See pages 78-79 for more on using online storage services.

TIDY YOUR DESKTOP

SORT YOUR ICONS USING STARDOCK FENCES

If your Windows Desktop is littered with shortcuts, folders and files, you may need some help to get it organised.

The free version of Stardock Fences (http://bit.ly/star261) tidies up all the items on your Desktop by creating fenced-off areas for the different

file types. The software can sort your icons automatically, or you can manually arrange everything yourself. Stardock Fences also lets you customise the layout and change the background style and colour. You can hide the fences and icons simply by double-clicking a blank area of the Desktop.

ORGANISE THE WINDOWS 7 START MENU

To customise the Programs menu, go to Start, right-click a blank area and select Properties. When the 'Taskbar and Start Menu' box opens, click the Customize button. You'll be able to change how

links, icons and menus look, and hide unwanted entries for features such as Control Panel, Documents, Default Programs and Help and Support.

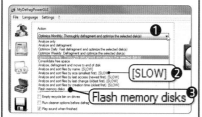

Defrag your hard disk using MyDefragPowerGUI

1 Launch MyDefragPowerGUI (www.wieldraaijer.nl), then go to Defragmentation Settings and choose an action from the drop-down menu ❶. Options marked as Slow ❷ can take a long time to complete, so you're better off choosing to optimise your system on a daily, weekly or monthly basis. The program can also optimise Flash drives ❸.

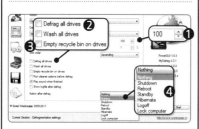

2 You can control the speed of the defragmentation process ❶, choose to defrag all drives ❷ and empty the Recycle Bin and clean up your computer ❸ before starting. You can also set what you want the program to do once the optimisation process has completed ❹. Click Start and the defragging window will open.

3 The Drive Selection icon ❶ lets you choose which disks to include. You can defrag, wash and empty the bin on each ❷. Advanced Settings ❸ lets you include or exclude files and run certain programs before or after a scan. You can configure the settings under Program Options ❹.

By default, Windows highlights newly installed programs, but you can disable this feature. The All Programs menu is sorted alphabetically by name, but this too can be changed. You can also adjust the number of recent programs that are listed. To get easy access to your favourite applications, right-click each one in turn under All Programs and select 'Pin to Start menu'.

TIDY THE WINDOWS 7 NOTIFICATION AREA

Programs often add icons to your System Tray that you might not necessarily want kept there. Windows 7 usually tucks these away inside a neat sub-menu, but it can still get pretty crowded over time.

Fortunately, it's easy to organise all the items in the tray. Right-click the Windows Taskbar, select Properties, then click the Customize button next to Notification Area. Use the drop-down menu next to each item and select whether you want to show the icon and notifications, hide the icon and notifications, or only show notifications.

REMOVE SHORTCUTS AND THE RECYCLE BIN

You can delete any Desktop shortcuts you don't require by selecting them and hitting the Delete key. When Windows asks you to confirm that you want to send each item to the Recycle Bin, click OK.

But what happens when you want to remove the Desktop shortcut for the bin itself? In Windows Vista, right-click the trash can icon and select Delete from the menu. In Windows 7, the process is a little more involved. Right-click the Desktop, select Personalize, then click the Change Desktop Icons link on the left. Untick the Recycle Bin box, and any other Desktop icons you don't want, and apply the change.

REMOVE UNWANTED ITEMS FROM THE RIGHT-CLICK MENU

When you right-click on a file on the Desktop, a menu appears offering a selection of options, including letting you scan the object with your anti-virus software, renaming it or deleting it.

Certain programs add their own entries to this menu, which can be annoying if you don't require them. You can remove these unwanted items using ShellNewHandler (http://shellnewhandler.sourceforge. net). This is a tiny 10KB utility that searches through the Registry for context menu entries and lets you get rid of any unnecessary ones.

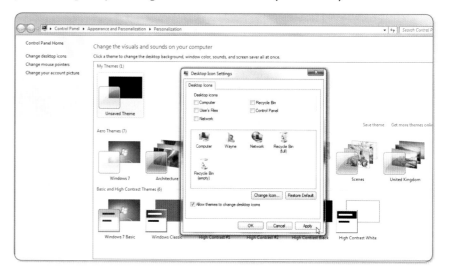

IDENTIFY AND FIX DISK ERRORS EARLY ON

Hard-disk problems can be catastrophic, so it's important to spot them as early as possible. Windows comes with its own error-checking tool called Chkdsk but there are some excellent free third-party programs available that do an even better job.

HDDScan (http://hddscan.com) is an excellent free diagnostic utility that can run S.M.A.R.T (Self-Monitoring, Analysis, and Reporting Technology) and surface scans, monitor a device's temperature and let you change certain disk parameters.

OPTIMISE YOUR HARD DISK BY DEFRAGMENTING IT

MyDefrag (www.mydefrag.com) is a speedy defragmenting tool that can reorder and optimise your hard disk. The program is easy to use – just select a script and start it running.

MyDefrag's interface is rather basic, so for something more sophisticated, give MyDefragPowerGUI (www.wieldraaijer. nl) a go. This new add-on provides an alternative front end for the tool and lets you choose the options you want from a drop-down menu, as well as schedule

defrags and clear out unwanted clutter. See our Mini Workshop opposite to find out how to use the program.

FIND AND FIX REGISTRY ERRORS SECURELY

Frequently installing, uninstalling and deleting programs can lead to errors in the Windows Registry, and these in turn can potentially cause your computer to slow down or crash.

Wise Registry Cleaner Free (http://bit. ly/wise261) scans the database for errors and then lets you fix them. You can choose which categories to include and the program will back up the Registry before making any changes to it.

BACK UP AND DEFRAGMENT YOUR REGISTRY

Ainvo Registry Defrag (www.ainvo.com/ en) analyses your Registry and evaluates its condition before defragging it. The process involves removing any unused spaces and reordering the data to make everything leaner and more efficient.

The tool saves a backup copy of the Registry to your hard disk before proceeding, just in case something goes wrong during the defrag.

SOLVE WINDOWS PROBLEMS AS AN ADMINISTRATOR

The System Maintenance Wizard can find and resolve a range of problems in Windows 7. Click Start, and type 'system maintenance' (without the quotes) into the box, then click 'Perform recommended System Maintenance tasks automatically'. Click the Advanced link and choose to run the troubleshooter as an Administrator – it's not absolutely necessary, but may unearth more errors this way.

You can also untick the option to apply repairs automatically if you'd prefer to see what changes are being proposed before they are implemented. Click Next to begin detecting issues, such as disk volume errors, broken shortcuts and unused Desktop icons.

CLEAN AND SPEED UP YOUR SYSTEM SIMULTANEOUSLY

360Amigo System Speedup (www.360amigo.com) is a general-purpose cleaning and system optimisation tool that can remove junk files, fix problems, defrag your hard disk and manage system startup.

It's incredibly easy to use: choose the options you want to include and then click the Start Scan button. Click the Problems Found link to view the errors the program has found and repair them.

The software also offers a wealth of useful system tools, including a duplicate file finder, file shredder, empty folder scanner and rootkit detector. See our Mini Workshop on page 88 to find out how to use 360Amigo.

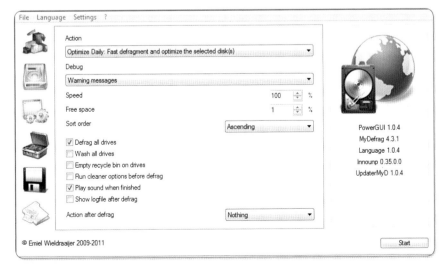

MINI WORKSHOP

Boost your system with 360Amigo

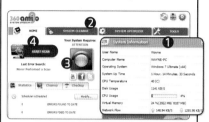

1 The home screen of 360Amigo (www.360amigo.com) provides some useful system information ➊, such as how long your computer has been on for and disk and CPU usage. Tabs along the top ➋ give you access to the program's features, and the traffic-light graphic ➌ shows you the overall status of your system. To clean your computer, click Start Scan. ➍

2 360Amigo will look for junk files and Registry errors, analyse your hard disk for fragmented files and check you're protected against tracking cookies and spyware. The number of problems ➊ always looks far worse than it is. Click any of the links to view the details and choose what to fix, then click Repair ➋.

3 System Cleaner ➊ gives access to the individual Junk Files, Registry Cleaner and Smart Defragmenter modules. You can also manage System Restore points here. The System Optimizer ➋ lets you control running processes and services and manage startup programs. Tools ➌ offers various useful system utilities.

SWEEP YOUR SYSTEM

GET TWO LAYERS OF MALWARE PROTECTION

To ensure your system is totally free from malware, it's worth running a full scan on a regular basis. Outpost Security Suite Free (www.agnitum.com) is a powerful free internet security suite with not one but two scanning engines. The first protects your system from viruses, while the second focuses on other threats, including spyware, adware and Trojans. The software also offers a personal firewall, safe surfing and anti-spam protection. There are separate 32- and 64-bit versions available, so make sure you download the correct one.

DETECT AND REMOVE HIDDEN MALWARE

Rootkits are one of the more sophisticated and annoying threats, and can be used to hide malicious software on your system. This makes them invisible and very difficult to find and remove. Most decent anti-virus programs can detect them, but if you want to be certain your system is free from infection, try running

NoVirusThanks Anti-Rootkit Free (http://bit.ly/root261). The free version of this powerful anti-rootkit program (which costs £12.37 to buy) detects hidden processes, stealth DLL modules and hidden drivers and keeps your PC clean of secret malware.

RUN THE MALICIOUS SOFTWARE REMOVAL TOOL

If you've ever looked at the list of available Windows Updates, you may have noticed that there's a Malicious Software Removal Tool. This is a program from Microsoft that's designed to identify and remove a number of common malware infections. If you don't already have the tool on your system, you can download it from http://bit.ly/mal261. The application gives you a choice of Quick, Full or Custom scans.

Although the Malicious Software Removal Tool provides a decent level of basic protection, you'll still need to have a good anti-virus/spyware tool installed.

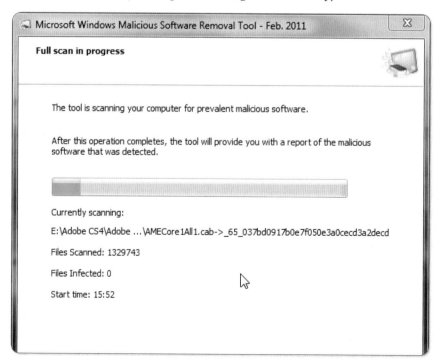

Best free
TOOLS TO REMOVE JUNK FILES

Don't waste your money on expensive clean-up software. Here are six programs that will improve your PC's performance for free

REMOVE EMPTY DIRECTORIES
www.jonasjohn.de/lab/red.htm
FILE SIZE: 395KB

Over time, your hard disk is likely to accumulate hundreds of empty folders left behind by uninstalled programs, deleted photos and accidental mouse-clicks. Remove Empty Directories (RED) lets you locate and remove these vacant directories quickly and easily. Any folders found by the tool can be reviewed before you delete them and you can choose to exempt certain directories.

WISE DISK CLEANER FREE
www.wisecleaner.com
FILE SIZE: 4.3MB

Combining a disk cleaner and a disk defragmenter, this excellent tool cleans and speeds up your system in a couple of minutes. Wise Disk Cleaner Free lets you delete temporary and junk files – even hidden ones – with a single click, and can be scheduled to run regularly at a time that suits you. Just remember to

deselect the Ask toolbar and homepage options during installation.

ERASETEMP
www.nodesoft.com/erasetemp
FILE SIZE: 124KB

This simple but useful tool automatically deletes temporary files from your system to prevent them from building up and hogging disk space. Just run EraseTemp and the program will remove all temporary files more than a day old as well as memory-dump files, which are created when Windows stops responding.

PC DECRAPIFIER
www.pcdecrapifier.com
FILE SIZE: 1.28MB

Clean-up tools generally remove clutter that's built up over time, but PC Decrapifier is designed for new PCs. The program gets rid of all the trial software, startup items and browser toolbars that come pre-installed on a new PC, and which can often slow it down from the start. You can choose exactly what to

uninstall and use the Restore Point function to recover from any problems.

BROWSER CLEANER
http://tcpmonitor.altervista.org
FILE SIZE: 898KB

Browsers pick up all sorts of rubbish from the web, but we often forget to clear them out. Browser Cleaner does the job for you and is especially useful if you use several different browsers. It lets you delete cookies, history and temporary internet files from Internet Explorer, Firefox, Chrome, Opera and Safari in one fell swoop. You can also erase your Flash and Java caches.

CLEANMEM
www.pcwintech.com/cleanmem
FILE SIZE: 1.07MB

To optimise your PC you need to free up memory as well as remove unwanted files. CleanMem improves Windows' memory management and keeps your system running smoothly by releasing any memory that's not being used.

MAKE MONEY ONLINE

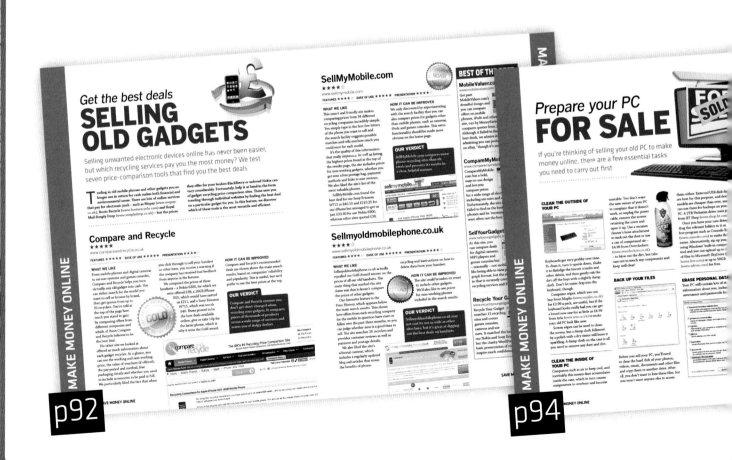

p96

Get the best deals
SELLING OLD GADGETS

Selling unwanted electronic devices online has never been easier, but which recycling services pay you the most money? We test seven price-comparison tools that find you the best deals

Trading in old mobile phones and other gadgets you no longer use in return for cash makes both financial and environmental sense. There are lots of online services that pay for electronic junk – such as Mopay (www.mopay. co.uk), Boots Recycle (www.bootsrecycle.com) and Royal Mail Simply Drop (www.simplydrop.co.uk) – but the prices they offer for your broken BlackBerry or unloved Nokia can vary considerably. Fortunately, help is at hand in the form of gadget-recycling price-comparison sites. These save you trawling through individual websites by finding the best deal on a particular gadget for you. In this feature, we discover which of these tools is the most versatile and efficient.

Compare and Recycle
★★★★★

www.compareandrecycle.co.uk

FEATURES ★★★★★   EASE OF USE ★★★★★   PRESENTATION ★★★★☆

WHAT WE LIKE
From mobile phones and digital cameras to sat-nav systems and games consoles, Compare and Recycle helps you turn virtually any old gadget into cash. You can either search for the model you want to sell or browse by brand, then get quotes from up to 33 recyclers. You're told at the top of the page how much you stand to gain by comparing offers from different companies and which of them Compare and Recycle believes to be the best deal.

No other site we looked at offered as much information about each gadget recycler. At a glance, you can see the working and non-working price, the value of vouchers (if offered), the pay period and method, free packaging details and whether you need to include accessories to be paid in full. We particularly liked the fact that when

you click through to sell your handset or other item, you receive a warning if the company has received bad feedback from anyone in the forums.

We compared the prices of three handsets – a Nokia 6300, for which we were offered £38; a 16GB iPhone 3GS, which would have netted us £211; and a Sony Ericsson W715, which was worth £40. These proved to be the best deals available online, give or take 10p for the latter phone, which is why it wins the Gold award.

HOW IT CAN BE IMPROVED
Compare and Recycle's recommended deals are shown above the main search results, based on companies' reliability and popularity. This is useful, but we'd prefer to see the best prices at the top.

OUR VERDICT
Compare and Recycle ensures you don't get short-changed when recycling your gadgets. It compares prices of thousands of products across a wide range of services and warns you of dodgy dealers.

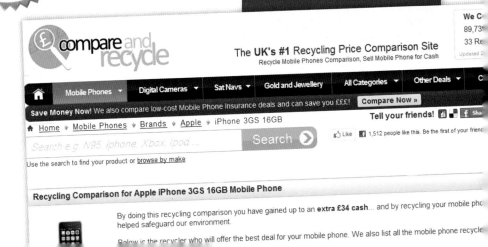

SellMyMobile.com

★★★★☆

www.sellmymobile.com

FEATURES ★★★★☆ EASE OF USE ★★★★★ PRESENTATION ★★★★☆

WHAT WE LIKE

This smart and friendly site makes comparing prices from 34 different recycling companies incredibly simple. You simply type in the first few letters of the phone you want to sell and the search facility suggests possible matches and tells you how much you could earn for each model.

It's the quality of this information that really impresses. As well as listing the highest prices found at the top of the results page, the site includes prices for non-working gadgets, whether you get sent a free postage bag, payment methods and links to user reviews. We also liked the site's list of the most valuable phones.

SellMyMobile.com found the best deal for our Sony Ericsson W715 at £40.10 and £210.25 for our iPhone but managed to get us just £33.60 for our Nokia 6300, whereas other sites quoted £38.

HOW IT CAN BE IMPROVED

We only discovered by experimenting with the search facility that you can also compare prices for gadgets other than mobile phones, such as cameras, iPods and games consoles. This extra functionality should be made more obvious on the home page.

OUR VERDICT

SellMyMobile.com compares more phone-recycling sites than its rivals and presents its results in a clear, helpful manner.

Sellmyoldmobilephone.co.uk

★★★★☆

www.sellmyoldmobilephone.co.uk

FEATURES ★★★★☆ EASE OF USE ★★★★★ PRESENTATION ★★★★☆

WHAT WE LIKE

Sellmyoldmobilephone.co.uk actually equalled our Gold Award winner on the prices of all our old handsets. The main thing that marked the site down was that it doesn't compare the prices of other gadgets.

Our favourite feature is the Price History, which appears below the main search results. This shows how offers from each recycling company for the mobile in question have risen or fallen over the past three months, so you can judge whether now is a good time to sell. The site searches 26 recyclers and provides customer reviews as well as payment and postage details.

We also liked the site's editorial content, which includes a regularly updated blog and articles that stress the benefits of phone-

recycling and instructions on how to delete data from your handset.

HOW IT CAN BE IMPROVED

The site could broaden its remit to include other gadgets. We'd also like to see prices for non-working phones included in the search results.

OUR VERDICT

Sellmyoldmobilephone.co.uk may not cast its net as wide as other sites here, but it's great at digging out the best deals on handsets.

BEST OF THE REST

MobileValuer.com

www.mobilevaluer.com

Get past MobileValuer.com's dreadful design and you can compare offers on mobile phones, iPods and other gadgets. The site, run by MoneySavingExpert.com, compares quotes from 20 companies. Although it failed to find us the best deals, we admire its honesty in admitting you can probably get more on eBay, "though it's more hassle".

CompareMyMobile.com

www.comparemymobile.com

CompareMyMobile. com has a bold, easy-to-use design and lets you compare prices for a wide range of electrical items, including sat-navs and computers. Unfortunately, the site consistently failed to find us the best prices for phones and its 'recommended' deals were often not the best available.

SellYourGadgets.co.uk

www.sellyourgadgets.co.uk

At this site, you can compare deals for digital cameras, MP3 players and games consoles but – unusually – not mobile phones. We like being able to view price trends in graph format, but the site is limited in that it currently covers just seven recycling services and 318 gadgets.

Recycle Your Gadget

www.recycleyourgadget.co.uk

Recycle Your Gadget searches 12 recycling sites and covers games consoles, cameras and sat-navs. It matched the best prices for our Nokia and Sony Ericsson phones, but the clunky WordPress design and basic presentation of results don't inspire much confidence.

MAKE MONEY ONLINE

Prepare your PC
FOR SALE

If you're thinking of selling your old PC to make money online, there are a few essential tasks you need to carry out first

CLEAN THE OUTSIDE OF YOUR PC

Keyboards get very grubby over time. To clean it, turn it upside down, shake it to dislodge the biscuit crumbs and other debris, and then gently rub the dirt off the keys with a slightly damp cloth. Don't let water drip into the keyboard, though.

Computer wipes, which you can buy from Maplin (www.maplin.co.uk) for £3.99 a pack, are useful, but if the keyboard looks really bad you can get a brand new one for as little as £4.99 from Aria (www.aria.co.uk) to make your old PC look like new.

Screen wipes can be used to clean the screen, but a damp cloth followed by a polish with a dry tissue will leave it sparkling. A damp cloth on the case is all you need to remove any dust and dirt.

CLEAN THE INSIDE OF YOUR PC

Computers suck in air to keep cool, and inevitably this means dust accumulates inside the case, which in turn causes components to overheat and become

unstable. You don't want the new owner of your PC to complain that it doesn't work, so unplug the power cable, remove the screws retaining the cover and open it up. Use a vacuum cleaner's hose attachment to suck out the dust or use a can of compressed air – £4.99 from Overclockers (www.overclockers.co.uk) – to blow out the dirt, but take care not to touch any components and keep well clear!

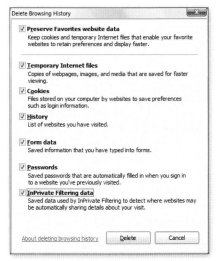

BACK UP YOUR FILES

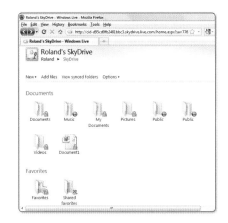

Before you sell your PC, you'll need to clear the hard disk of your photos, videos, music, documents and other files and copy them to another drive. After all, you don't want to lose these files, but you won't want anyone else to access

them either. External USB disk drives are best for this purpose, and desktop models are cheaper than ever, and you can use them for backups on your new PC. A 2TB Verbatim drive costs just £80 from BT Shop (www.shop.bt.com).

Once you have your new drive, simply drag the relevant folders to it or use a free program such as Comodo Backup (www.comodo.com) to make things easier. Alternatively, zip up your folders using Windows' built-in compression tool and you can upload up to 25GB of files to Microsoft SkyDrive (http://home.live.com) or up to 50GB to ADrive (www.adrive.com) for free.

ERASE PERSONAL DATA

Your PC will contain lots of stored information about you, including usernames and passwords for websites,

online stores and banking, email contacts and so on. These should be removed before you sell your PC or someone else could use your identity.

Free programs such as CCleaner (www.ccleaner.com) and Free Internet Window Washer (www.eusing.com) are useful for this purpose, while Eraser (http://eraser.heidi.ie) will overwrite sensitive files for extra security.

You should also remove usernames and passwords stored in your web browser. In Internet Explorer, select Delete Browsing History from the Safety menu and tick everything. In Firefox, go to Tools, Options, Security, click Saved Passwords, then click Remove All.

DEAUTHORISE ITUNES

Your iTunes store (http://itunes.apple.com/gb) account can be used on only five computers, so before you sell a PC you should deauthorise it first. If you don't and you've set up your account on several machines, the sixth PC you use won't play purchased music and videos.

To deauthorise your iTunes account on your old PC, go to the Store menu

and select Deauthorize Account. You can then install iTunes on your new computer and authorise it by going to Store, Authorize Computer.

SCAN YOUR PC FOR VIRUSES

You don't want to pass on a PC that's infected, so you should scan it for viruses, spyware and other types of malware before you sell it on.

There are lots of free online tools available for checking the health of your computer without you needing to download any software other than a small plug-in. Our favourite is ESET Online Scanner (www.eset.com/online-scanner), but you could also try Trend Micro HouseCall (http://housecall.trendmicro.com) for a second opinion.

REMOVE ANY SOFTWARE YOU'VE BOUGHT

If your computer contains hundreds of pounds worth of software, you have to ask yourself whether you want to pass it on with the computer or not. The PC may command a higher price if it has some good software on it, but you probably won't get back all the money you've paid over the years.

If the software isn't part of the deal, you should uninstall it using

the free version of Revo Uninstaller (www.revouninstaller.com). It's wise to uninstall commercial programs anyway because they're licensed to you and may contain your name and other details, which could spell trouble if the next owner uses the machine for illegal purposes.

SCAN THE HARD DISK FOR ERRORS

After uninstalling software, removing your music, videos, photos and documents, and cleaning up your web and Windows tracks, you should check that the hard disk is free of errors.

To do this in Windows 7 or Vista, click Start, Computer and right-click on the disk. Select Properties from the menu and click Check Now under Error-checking on the Tools tab.

In Windows XP, right-click on the hard disk in My Computer to access this tool. Select the option 'Automatically fix file system errors' and click Start.

RETURN THE PC TO ITS FACTORY STATE

Your computer may have been supplied with recovery discs that restore the system to the state it was in when it was built. More commonly, you're prompted to burn recovery discs when you first switch on a new PC.

If you have recovery discs, you should consider using them because this will wipe the system clean and reinstall all the right drivers. However, they'll work only if you haven't changed the hardware since you bought the PC.

Earn money by
WRITING REVIEWS

Consumer-review sites let you read other people's opinions of products and services – and you can earn money by sharing your own thoughts. Here we give our verdict on seven popular review communities

Ciao
★★★★★
www.ciao.co.uk

FEATURES ★★★★★   EASE OF USE ★★★★★   PRESENTATION ★★★★☆

WHAT WE LIKE

Ciao is now part of the Microsoft stable, and uses the company's Bing search engine, which is very much to its benefit. Whereas some of Ciao's rivals, such as Dooyoo, struggle to present accurate results for product searches, Ciao reliably and repeatedly found us the right goods. It's an important benefit, because if it takes too long to find specific product reviews, you're likely to simply give up.

Ciao has a plentiful stock of reviews, with popular products attracting dozens – sometimes hundreds – of user evaluations. Even the more unlikely items benefit; we found a detailed synopsis for York Fruits sweets, for example. So, if you need personal buying advice on just about anything, Ciao is the place to find it. Readers can rate reviews from 'exceptional' to 'not helpful' as a quality-control measure.

Related to these scores is the potential to earn money by penning reviews of your own. We say 'potential' because you shouldn't entertain any notions of securing fortunes here. However, write an appreciated review of a popular product and Ciao will credit you with up to a couple of pennies for each positive reader rating. Notch up a fiver's worth and it will be credited to your bank account.

HOW IT CAN BE IMPROVED

An obvious improvement would be for Ciao to offer payment via PayPal, as other review sites do. As it stands, if you want to make a bit of pocket money from writing your own product reviews, you need to supply Ciao with your bank account details – and that just seems a bit dated.

OUR VERDICT

Ciao has a huge database of quality consumer reviews and is therefore a substantial and valuable resource for shoppers. Writers will also like Ciao's (mostly) clear payment policy and low payout threshold – but don't consider it a career move.

MAKE MONEY ONLINE

Dooyoo
★★★★☆

www.dooyoo.co.uk

FEATURES ★★★★☆   EASE OF USE ★★★★☆   PRESENTATION ★★★★★

WHAT WE LIKE

Dooyoo is more inviting than Ciao and looks like a consumer-review site rather than just another price-comparison site.

Like Ciao, it lets reviewers profit from their work, but instead of pennies, the site pays 'dooyooMiles'. There are numerous intricacies to this currency but, ultimately, dooyooMiles don't add up to a hill of beans. Hundreds of them can be 'earned' for a single review, along with extra dooyooMiles for each reader thumbs-up, but you'll need to amass 50,000 dooyooMiles to cash them in for £50. Alternatively, they can be exchanged for Amazon vouchers or given to charity.

As for the reviews, the visitor-rating quality control ensures that opinions posted on Dooyoo are as good as those on Ciao. This means that, over time, the most useful reviews naturally rise to top.

HOW IT CAN BE IMPROVED

Dooyoo's search system is a bit hit and miss. Search for 'iPhone 4', for example, and it appears several rungs down the results ladder. The points-based payment programme is more complex than it need be, and the pay-out threshold is much higher than Ciao's £5.

OUR VERDICT

Dooyoo hosts a vast database of reviews and is well presented, but the ropey search tool and dooyouMiles are turn-offs.

Epinions.com
★★★★☆

www.epinions.com

FEATURES ★★★★☆   EASE OF USE ★★★★☆   PRESENTATION ★★★★☆

WHAT WE LIKE

Epinions.com is part of Shopping.com, which is part of eBay. If you're serious about earning money from writing reviews, it may be reassuring to commit to a site that's backed by a web giant.

Epinions.com is simply but cleanly presented and well-organised. To find a review, use the search box or drill down through the categories and click the Read Reviews button or tab, as appropriate.

Signing up as a reviewer is simple: fill in a registration form, click the emailed verification link and off you go. An account-summary page shows how much you've earnt. However, the mechanics of the site's earning system aren't clear; the company states its formula "must remain vague" in order to prevent scammers.

HOW IT CAN BE IMPROVED

Non-US residents have to jump through hoops to claim their Epinions.com earnings. Some of these obstacles are legal requirements beyond the service's control, but others – such as the $100 (around £62) payment threshold – could be improved.

OUR VERDICT

Epinions.com's US focus isn't a problem when you're writing reviews, but the payout procedure for contributors is convoluted.

BEST OF THE REST

MyLot

www.mylot.com

MyLot isn't so much a consumer-review site as a place where you can waffle on about almost any topic imaginable. Should your thoughts strike a chord with enough users, a few pennies are paid as a reward. However, MyLot's payment scheme is clouded by smoke and mirrors.

Review Stream

www.reviewstream.com

This site promises attractive payments for each review – up to $2.50 (about £1.55) when we visited – but we're not convinced people are earning fortunes. While there are thousands of reviews, the payment criteria are vague and the guidelines on submissions are far from plain.

SharedReviews

www.sharedreviews.com

SharedReviews describes itself as a social network for aspiring writers and has a 'cash rewards pool' that evenly distributes the amount earned by its members from their reviews and articles each month. Sadly, the site is a mess and it's hard to find a review of a particular product.

Shvoong.com

www.shvoong.com

Shvoong requests that you restrict your contributions to 900-word critiques of books, newspaper articles, websites and movies. It also has a clear payment policy: 10 per cent of the site's ad revenue is shared with writers, divided by popularity. Unfortunately, a fractional share of 10 per cent of what's likely to be very little will probably add up to hardly anything.

MUSIC & VIDEO

p104

Watch
FREE FILMS ONLINE

Whether you're into old classics, animation or blockbusters, there are lots of places to watch movies online legally. Here are 10 of the best

WATCH CLASSIC MOVIES

www.classiccinemaonline.com

If you want to enjoy great films from yesteryear, then head to Classic Cinema Online. This site features hundreds of old films from the silent era, the Golden Age of Hollywood and beyond, neatly categorised into genres such as comedy, drama, romance, sci-fi and westerns.

As you'd expect from such old material, the quality varies and the site can be slow to load. But we like the options to share videos on social networks and to post comments and requests on the blog. You can also view short films and old newsreels.

SAMPLE FILMS: Alfred Hitchcock's *The Ring, Zorro's Black Whip*

ENJOY QUALITY DRAMA

www.blinkbox.com/Movies/Free

There's nothing like getting your teeth into a good drama, and at Blinkbox

you can watch 150 of them for free. Drama is by far the largest of the site's 14 categories, followed by comedy, and it includes a host of movies featuring big names, such as *Barfly*, with Mickey Rourke as an alcoholic poet, *My Left Foot*, with Daniel Day-Lewis, and *The Addiction*, starring Christopher Walken.

SAMPLE FILMS: *Lantana, Distant Voices, Still Lives*

WATCH FREEVIEW FILMS ONLINE

www.tvcatchup.com

TVCatchup offers live streaming of dozens of Freeview channels including Channel 4's Film4 (www.film4.com), which screens everything from cult classics to recent blockbusters. You can also watch Movies4Men (www.movies4men.co.uk) and stream films as they're being shown on the BBC, ITV and Five. You need to register to

use TVCatchup, but this is free and the service can also be accessed on your iPhone or iPad. The picture quality is excellent and the streaming reliable.

SAMPLE FILMS: *Cloverfield, Shallow Grave*

SHORT COMEDY FILMS

www.atom.com

This site began as Atom Films, a showcase for short films that brought Aardman's popular stop-animation series *Angry Kid* to wider attention. Today, Atom.com is a full-blown comedy network that features spoofs,

extreme humour and 'sci-fi and horror hilarity', among other genres.

The offerings are usually short so you can dip in and out at your leisure, while picture quality is high and each video can be rated, shared and embedded on your website or blog. Be prepared for some fruity language, though.

SAMPLE FILMS: *Quitters, Claymation Star Trek*

WATCH A DOCUMENTARY

www.freedocumentaries.org
Free Documentaries has hundreds of compelling films to watch online for nothing. These range from familiar titles such as *Super Size Me* to more obscure films such as *Orwell Rolls in His Grave*, an examination of US political corruption.

The site features diverse content, offering documentaries in Spanish and French as well as English, and has a handy 'Films by Topic' menu. You can select the screen size – small, medium or large – and watch a preview in an embedded YouTube window before playing the full movie.

SAMPLE FILMS: *Sicko, The Road to Guantanamo*

WATCH MOVIES ON YOUTUBE

www.youtube.com/movies
Thanks to a 2010 deal with Blinkbox, you can now watch hundreds of free full-length films on YouTube. The Films

section features everything from the animated Orwell classic *Animal Farm* to full-on action with Jackie Chan.

There's an air of the bargain basement about many of the titles, but it's still a great way to see a Bollywood film, check out a wealth of horror movies and laugh along to dozens of comedy flicks.

SAMPLE FILMS: *Night of the Living Dead, Cathy Come Home*

WATCH OLD FILM NOIR MOVIES

www.archive.org/details/Film_Noir
The Internet Archive (www.archive. org) has a wide selection of free films to watch online, including an excellent Film Noir section. The site features 77 film noir titles from the 1940s and 1950s, including the classic *D.O.A.* and Johnny Cash in the little-known but intriguing-sounding *Door-to-Door Maniac*. Films can be streamed online or downloaded to your computer.

SAMPLE FILMS: *Impact, Panic in the Streets*

ENJOY SOME LOW-BUDGET MOVIES

www.imovietube.com
Thanks to the internet, you can check out films that never made it as far as DVD or television in the UK, let alone the cinema. At iMovieTube, you can view a host of independent movies and specialist titles for free.

The films span a wide variety of genres, including horror, musical and fantasy, and they stream quickly in your browser, although you do have to tolerate a large logo in the bottom left-hand corner. While there are some real stinkers, such as *Manos: The Hands of Fate* – said to be the worst movie of all time – others are definitely worth watching, if only for a laugh.

SAMPLE FILMS: *Big Buck Bunny, Dead Man Drinking*

STREAM A BLOCKBUSTER ONLINE

www.lovefilm.com
One of the best places to watch mainstream films online is at LoveFilm – but there's a catch. The selection of free titles available for non-subscribers is woeful. However, if you subscribe to the DVD-rental service for £9.99 per month, you get free access to loads of top Hollywood films online such as *Batman Begins* and *Planet of the Apes*, as well as foreign titles such as *Let the Right One In*. The streaming quality is excellent and you can view each title full-screen.

SAMPLE FILMS: *The Machinist, The Third Man*

WATCH OLD ROMANTIC FAVOURITES

www.jaman.com/movies/free-movies
Have your tissues at the ready when you watch Jaman's free selection of romantic films. These include full-length movies such as *Charade* (starring Audrey Hepburn and Cary Grant) and the 1947 John Wayne flick *Angel and the Badman*. Videos can be embedded on your website, blog or social-networking page, and there are lots of community reviews to ensure you don't waste your time on a turkey.

SAMPLE FILMS: *Stagecoach, Wanderlust*

Best free sites for
STREAMING MUSIC

Which free music-streaming sites have the most songs and the best tools? We test seven popular services to bring music to your ears

....

Grooveshark
★★★★★

http://listen.grooveshark.com

EASE OF USE ★★★★★ FEATURES ★★★★★ VARIETY ★★★★★ QUALITY ★★★★★

....

WHAT WE LIKE

The best thing about Grooveshark is that it lets you play unlimited tracks for free. You can add the ones you like to the My Library feature, which has a limit of 500 'favourites' and 5,000 songs.

Apart from the adverts that dominate the right-hand side of the layout, we love the clarity of the interface and the fact that Grooveshark's main focus is to help you find and listen to music. It's also wonderfully easy to manage the songs you choose from the huge library, which the site claims includes 22 million tracks, especially compared to some of the more complicated services reviewed in this test.

You don't even have to register to use Grooveshark. Even without registering, however, the site thoughtfully stores the songs you place in your playlist so you can access them quickly the next time you visit. It's simple to search for tracks and share them via Facebook, Twitter and email,

and there's a widget for embedding tracks and playlists in a blog or web page. You can also listen to playlists created by other users and instantly sort them by track name, artist or album. All these features are free, but you can pay $6 (about £3.70) per month to access Grooveshark from a mobile device or Desktop widget. This subscription service ditches the ads and instead of limiting the size of your library to 500 favourites and 5,000 songs, you can have as many as you like.

HOW IT CAN BE IMPROVED

It's hard to see how Grooveshark can be improved without changing the free-to-stream business model and dumping the ads. We'd like to see more album artwork and a pop-out music player, but really that's nitpicking.

OUR VERDICT

Grooveshark has a huge library of songs and albums and is ingeniously organised. If you want to listen to unlimited music for free, this is the service for you.

SAVE MONEY ONLINE

Spotify

★★★★★

www.spotify.com

EASE OF USE ★★★★★   FEATURES ★★★★☆   VARIETY ★★★★★   QUALITY ★★★★★

WHAT WE LIKE

We reviewed the Open version of Spotify, which lets you stream up to 20 hours of free music per month, supported by ads. The Free version offers unlimited streaming but requires an invite from a Premium member.

Spotify's super-slick interface is a joy to use for beginners and veterans in all its versions, and it's as easy as pie to install the Spotify Desktop software.

It's easy to find and play music (there are around 10 million tracks to choose from) or dig deeper to set up playlists and libraries. It's also easy to import music from your PC and share playlists with friends using the Facebook links. Spotify is the most comprehensive music-streaming service we've used and it had every track we searched for, no matter how obscure, but the listening limit imposed by the Open version places it behind the unlimited Gooveshark.

HOW IT CAN BE IMPROVED

We understand the Open service has to be paid for with adverts, but why so many? It should be easier to get an invite, and increasing the Open version to 30 hours a month would be welcome, too.

OUR VERDICT

Spotify is still an excellent service, with a rich library of tracks. It's a shame about the 20-hour-per-month limitation for the Open version and those pesky ads.

Jango

★★★★☆

www.jango.com

EASE OF USE ★★★★☆   FEATURES ★★★★☆   VARIETY ★★★☆☆   QUALITY ★★★★☆

WHAT WE LIKE

Jango avoids the pitfalls of other sites we tested by concentrating on what it's good at: providing a simple music-streaming service that lets you search for specific artists and create playlists of similar acts.

There's plenty more if you want it, including a 500,000-song library, artist photos and biographies, links to YouTube videos and details of similar bands that are liked by other members. Register with the site and you can save the radio stations you create rather than just compile them as you go, add new artists manually and ban those you don't want to hear. You can also tune into what other people are listening to and even become their 'Jango friend'. The sign-up process is short and sweet and the user-friendly homepage lets you swap messages easily with other Jango members.

HOW IT CAN BE IMPROVED

Using Jango would be a more pleasant experience if it stopped pestering you with a registration window and let you sign up when you're ready. It would also be useful if the music player could be popped out in a standalone window and if the site didn't seem to disappear off the bottom of the page.

OUR VERDICT

Jango has the smallest library of our top three sites, but it's still great for hassle-free listening. The site has a surprising number of mainstream songs and gives handy recommendations of similar artists.

BEST OF THE REST

Last.fm

www.last.fm

What has happened to Last.fm? The site put lots of effort into its 'scrobbling' sharing and recommendation feature, but its song library has deteriorated sharply. Some tracks play in full, some play 30-second clips and others don't play at all. Disappointing.

We7

www.we7.com

We like We7 a lot. It has a swish interface, an extensive free music library and loads of useful features. However, the adverts that play before every track are a constant distraction and mean it just misses out on a top-three placing.

Deezer

www.deezer.com

With its smart, simple interface and strong community features, French site Deezer certainly looks promising. Sadly, nearly all of our searches for mainstream artists produced a selection of cover and karaoke versions.

MySpace Music

www.myspace.com/music

MySpace Music is frustratingly disorganised and the design makes your head hurt, but it's still a great way to hear unusual and unsigned bands and solo artists. Many tracks are free to download as well as stream online.

Best free
VIDEO-EDITING TOOLS

Great home movies don't have to cost a fortune. Here are 12 free tools available from the web for editing and enhancing your videos

WINDOWS LIVE MOVIE MAKER 2011

http://explore.live.com
Microsoft removed its Movie Maker video-editor from Windows 7 to keep the operating system as streamlined as possible, but it can be quickly restored with this free download. Windows Live Movie Maker 2011 employs Microsoft's love-it-or-loathe-it ribbon interface, so all functions are contained within tabs or accessed via the customisable Quick Access Toolbar at the top.

More advanced tools include the ability to fade soundtracks and apply a variety of artistic effects. We also like the AutoMovie option, which essentially makes a movie for you, complete with music, transitions and fades. Note that Live Movie Maker 2011 works with Vista and Windows 7, but not XP.

JAYCUT

http://jaycut.com
JayCut is a video-editing tool with such excellent production values that it's easy

to forget that it's entirely web-based. While the charcoal interface owes plenty to Adobe Premiere – the top video-editing choice for professionals – JayCut is instantly accessible to beginners.

Tabs provide quick access to both content (videos, images and audio) and post-production tools, such as transitions and captions, and you can even record new material using a camera or microphone attached to your PC.

PINNACLE VIDEOSPIN

www.videospin.com/uk
VideoSpin is a free video-editing package from the same company that makes the popular Pinnacle Studio software. Although the tool doesn't have all the advanced features of its paid-for stablemate, it provides versatile timeline-based editing, with lots of built-in transitions and caption styles.

Finished movies can be output in a variety of popular formats, including AVI and MPEG. However, although MPEG2, MPEG4 and DivX codecs are

supplied, they're on a trial basis only. If you want to continue using them after 15 days, it will cost you £6.99.

YOUTUBE EDITOR

www.youtube.com/editor
Few people realise that YouTube has a built-in video-editing facility. It's pretty basic – particularly on the audio front, where only YouTube-approved music tracks are available as soundtrack overlays – but for the simple cutting and splicing of your own YouTube videos, it's as convenient as can be.

There are a handful of transitions that can be applied, and videos can be rotated at the click of a button – a particularly useful feature in the context of YouTube, where uploads are often performed directly from smartphones.

VLC MEDIA PLAYER

www.videolan.org
Sometimes you'll find yourself using a video-editing tool for the sole purpose of improving playback – perhaps the

original footage is too dark or the audio is slightly out of sync with the pictures. In such situations, you can save a lot of time by forgoing editing completely and instead using VLC Media Player to process the footage on the go. From fixing the aspect ratio to turning movies into a tile puzzle, VLC is capable of carrying out pretty much any video-editing task worth doing.

AVIDEMUX
http://fixounet.free.fr/avidemux
Avidemux describes itself as suitable for 'simple cutting, filtering and encoding tasks'. However, don't read 'simple' as meaning easy: while Avidemux is certainly fast and effective in the right hands, it can take a while to get to grips with the program's quirky interface.

It's worth persevering, though, because there are dozens of nifty filters on offer and the 'scrubber' tool that removes unwanted elements is one of the best we've ever seen.

VIRTUALDUB
www.virtualdub.org
VirtualDub is a linear video-processing tool that's designed for people who need to apply similar changes to large numbers of videos. By this token, VirtualDub is a little trickier to master than other tools here because it assumes that users have a certain level

of knowledge about video processing. It even has a built-in hex editor for analysing parts of video files that won't play properly, for example.

FREEMAKE VIDEO CONVERTER
www.freemake.com
If Avidemux and VirtualDub make good bedfellows for video-editing experts, then Freemake Video Converter is the best program for video novices to get started with. The big, colourful buttons carry clear descriptions of functions (such as 'to DVD' and 'to YouTube'), and the interface steers clear of jargon.

The upshot is that Freemake demands no specialist knowledge to convert videos from one format to another, which makes it extremely easy to use and very useful for beginners.

HANDBRAKE
http://handbrake.fr
HandBrake is a no-nonsense source-to-destination video-processing tool. The interface is very simple, especially the tabbed design of the output settings, which makes the program easier to navigate than other similar tools. HandBrake also includes a dozen or so preset output profiles, although these are mainly useful only for playing back footage on Apple devices.

DVD SHRINK
www.dvdshrink.org
DVD Shrink has been around for ages, and its longevity is down to an ability to do one thing really well: that is to take DVD movie discs and shrink the contents down so they will fit on to a standard 4.7GB single-sided DVD-R disc.

This can be achieved using other video-editing programs and enhancement tools mentioned in this feature, but the difference with DVD Shrink is that it requires no specialist

knowledge – the job is under way in a couple of clicks. It's also possible to re-author discs, so you can remove unwanted chapters.

DVD Shrink works only with DVDs and not Blu-ray discs, and remember the usual legal provisos about copying and distributing copyrighted material.

TMPGENC FREE
http://tmpgenc.pegasys-inc.com
If you'd like to convert digital video to MPEG for use on VCDs, SVCDs and DVDs, try TMPGEnc Free. Novices can use the program's Project Wizard to get the job done with very little technical know-how, while expert users can build a batch list of transcoding tasks before leaving TMPGEnc to perform the conversions.

The program can also manage MPEG2 transcoding, although this is disabled after 30 days unless you pay $37 (about £23) to upgrade to the full version.

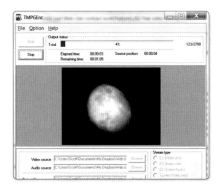

MPEG STREAMCLIP
www.squared5.com
Rather like VLC Media Player, MPEG Streamclip seems able to deal with any type of video file thrown at it. Admittedly, it isn't the simplest tool to use, but we've included the program here because it has a useful batch-processing facility, so the same set of edits/changes can be applied to multiple video clips simultaneously.

SECURITY WORKSHOPS

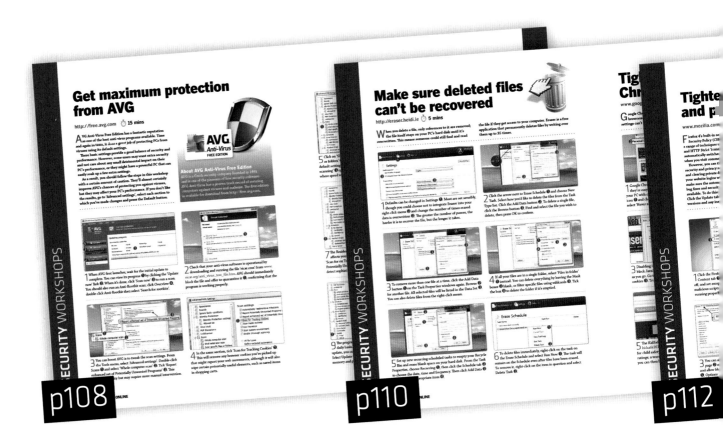

Surf anonymously using a proxy server

Walln: http://walln.com ⏱ 5 mins

Encrypt your entire PC

TrueCrypt: www.truecrypt.org ⏱ 10 mins

p114

Get maximum protection from AVG

http://free.avg.com   15 mins

AVG Anti-Virus Free Edition has a fantastic reputation as one of the best anti-virus programs available. Time and again in tests, it does a great job of protecting PCs from viruses using its default settings.

These basic settings provide a good balance of security and performance. However, some users may want extra security and not care about any small detrimental impact on their PC's performance, or they might have a powerful PC that can easily soak up a few extra settings.

As a result, you should follow the steps in this workshop with a certain amount of caution. They'll almost certainly improve AVG's chances of protecting you against viruses, but they may affect your PC's performance. If you don't like the results, go to 'Advanced settings', select each section to which you've made changes and press the Default button.

About AVG Anti-Virus Free Edition

AVG is a Czech security company founded in 1991 and is one of the pioneers of free security software. AVG Anti-Virus has a proven track record of securing computers against viruses and malware. The free edition is available for download from http://free.avg.com.

1 When AVG first launches, wait for the initial update to complete. You can view its progress ❶ by clicking the 'Update now' link ❷. When it's done, click 'Scan now' ❸ to run a scan. You should also run an Anti-Rootkit scan; click Overview ❹, double-click Anti-Rootkit then select 'Search for rootkits'.

2 Check that your anti-virus software is operational by downloading and running the file 'eicar.com' from www. eicar.org/anti_virus_test_file.htm. AVG should immediately block the file and offer to quarantine it ❶, confirming that the program is working properly.

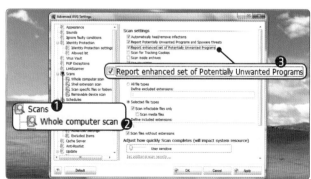

3 You can boost AVG is to tweak the scan settings. From the Tools menu, select 'Advanced settings'. Double-click Scans ❶ and select 'Whole computer scan' ❷. Tick 'Report enhanced set of Potentially Unwanted Programs' ❸. This increases security but may require more manual intervention.

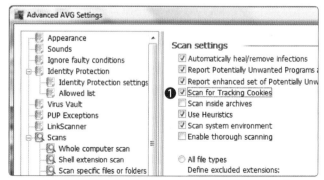

4 In the same section, tick 'Scan for Tracking Cookies' ❶. This will remove any browser cookies you've picked up that might report your web movements, although it will also wipe certain potentially useful elements, such as saved items in shopping carts.

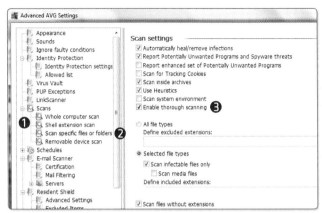

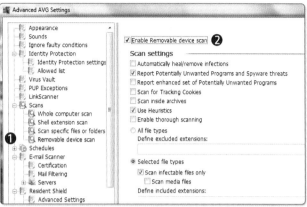

5 Click on 'Shell extension scan' ❶ or 'Scan specific files or folders' ❷. Both have the same options but different default settings. You may want to select the 'Enable thorough scanning' ❸ option, but only in 'Scan specific files or folders', where speed will be less of an issue.

6 'Removable device scan' ❶ is turned off by default. This performs a scan every time you plug in a USB device, so is worth turning on ❷ if your computer is often exposed to USB devices shared with external computers, particularly public ones such as those in schools or libraries.

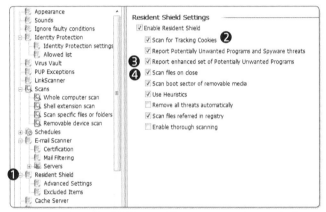

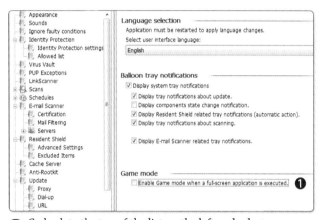

7 The Resident Shield ❶ scans files as you use them, which affects your PC's performance. You should also turn on 'Scan for on Tracking Cookies' ❷ and 'Report enhanced set of Potentially Unwanted Programs' ❸. 'Scan files on close' ❹ may detect sophisticated viruses.

8 Go back to the top of the list on the left and select Appearance. Untick 'Enable Game mode when a full-screen application is executed' ❶, particularly if you're not a gamer. This allows threat messages through, even when you're running full-screen applications.

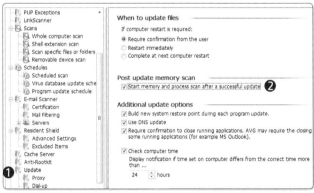

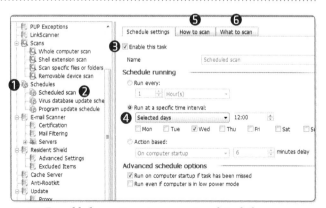

9 The program is already set up to download updates on a daily basis. If your software has performed a successful update, you can set it to perform a quick automatic scan. Select Update ❶ on the left, then tick the box next to 'Start memory and process scan after a successful update' ❷.

10 For added security, set up a post-update daily scan of your whole PC. Double-click Schedules ❶, then 'Scheduled scan' ❷. On the 'Schedule settings' tab select 'Enable this task' ❸ and choose when you want the scan to run ❹. You can tweak the options in 'How to scan' ❺ and 'What to scan' ❻.

Make sure deleted files can't be recovered

http://eraser.heidi.ie ⏱ 5 mins

When you delete a file, only references to it are removed; the file itself stays on your PC's hard disk until it's overwritten. This means someone could still find and read the file if they get access to your computer. Eraser is a free application that permanently deletes files by writing over them up to 35 times.

1 Defaults can be changed in Settings ❶. Most are set sensibly, though you could choose not to integrate Eraser into your right-click menu ❷ and change the number of times erased data is overwritten ❸. The greater the number of passes, the harder it is to recover the file, but the longer it takes.

2 Click the arrow next to Erase Schedule ❶ and choose New Task. Select how you'd like to delete the files from the Task Type list. Click the Add Data button ❷. To delete a single file, click the Browse button ❸. Find and select the file you wish to delete, then press OK to confirm.

3 To remove more than one file at a time, click the Add Data button ❶ on the Task Properties windows again. Browse ❷ for another file. All selected files will be listed in the Data Set ❸. You can also delete files from the right-click menu.

4 If all your files are in a single folder, select 'Files in folder' ❶ instead. You can delete everything by leaving the Mask boxes ❷ blank, or filter specific files using wildcards ❸. Tick the box ❹ to delete the folder if it's emptied.

5 Set up new recurring scheduled tasks to empty your Recycle Bin and erase blank space on your hard disk. From the Task Properties, choose Recurring ❶, then click the Schedule tab ❷ to choose the date, time and frequency. Then click Add Data ❸ and select the appropriate item ❹.

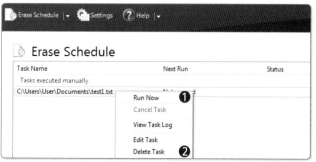

6 To delete files immediately, right-click on the task on the Erase Schedule and select Run Now ❶. The task will remain on the Schedule even after files have been erased. To remove it, right-click on the item in question and select Delete Task ❷.

Tighten up Google Chrome's security

www.google.com/chrome ⏱ 10 mins

Google Chrome may be one of the most secure web browsers available, but that doesn't mean its security settings can't be improved. In this workshop, we'll look at ways in which you can tighten up Chrome's built-in security settings, and also show you how to install and use some security-boosting extensions.

1 Google Chrome can save passwords on any site you visit, but they're easy to view so it can be a security risk if you share your PC with others. To disable this function, click the Spanner icon ❶ and choose Options. Under the Personal Stuff tab ❷ select 'Never save passwords' ❸ and Close ❹.

2 Chrome blocks pop-ups by default, but you can allow them on some sites. Click the icon in the address bar ❶ and select 'Always allow pop-ups from' ❷. To remove the site, go back to Options and select the 'Under the hood' tab. Choose 'Content settings', Pop-ups and Exceptions.

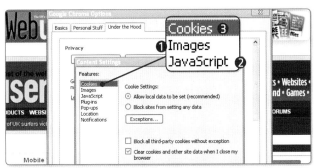

3 Disabling images ❶ is a bit extreme, but you may want to block JavaScript and cookies, letting trusted sites through as you go. Go to 'Content settings' to block JavaScript ❷ and cookies ❸. Trusted sites can be added in the same way as Step 2.

4 The McAfee Site Advisor extension (http://bit.ly/mcafee261) scans sites for potential threats. A tick icon ❶ denotes a safe site, a cross means a threat is detected. You can manage options and notifications through Tools ❷, Extensions ❸.

5 The KidSafe LinkExtend extension (http://bit.ly/kidsafe261) blocks unsuitable content and gives ratings for child safety on each site. Click the icon ❶ to display the ratings; a warning appears if a site contains adult content and you can then block it.

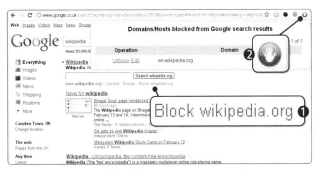

6 Use the Personal Blocklist extension (http://bit.ly/blocklist261) to block certain domains or hosts in Google searches. Once it's installed, click the Block link ❶ under a result to block it in future searches. To unblock or edit sites you've blocked, click the hand icon ❷ next to the address bar.

Tighten up Firefox 4's security and privacy settings

www.mozilla.com ⏱ 15 mins

Firefox 4's built-in security features include Content Security Policy (CSP), which detects and prevents against a range of techniques used by hackers to steal information, and HTTP Strict Transport Security (HSTS), which automatically switches you to the encrypted version of a site when you visit commerce sites such as PayPal.

However, you can tighten things further by tweaking the security and privacy settings. It's worth managing cookies and clearing private data, for example, as well as protecting your website logins with a master password. You should also make sure the automatic updates feature is turned on, so any bug fixes and security patches are installed as soon they're available. To do this, go to Options and click Advanced. Click the Update tab and make sure it's set to download new versions and any installed add-ons automatically.

About Firefox 4
The latest version of Mozilla's browser launched in March 2011. It was originally due to be launched in 2010, but was delayed because of problems discovered during testing.

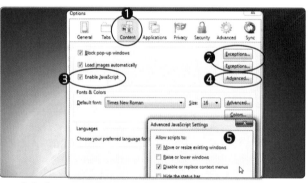

1 Click the Firefox button, select Options and click the Content tab ❶. You can toggle the pop-up blocker on or off, and set exceptions ❷. Disabling JavaScript ❸ can stop malicious scripts but will prevent web apps such as Gmail from running properly. Click Advanced ❹ to set script functions ❺.

2 A better way to manage JavaScript is to install the NoScript add-on (http://bit.ly/practical1252), which disables any potentially dangerous executable content. By default, it blocks all scripts on all pages, so you need to customise it. Click Options ❶ or right-click the NoScript icon ❷.

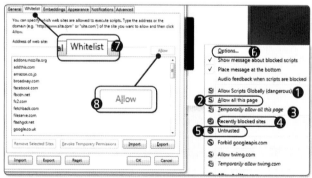

3 You can allow all scripts ❶, permit them on the current page ❷ or temporarily permit them ❸. You can also view and allow blocked items ❹ and mark dodgy sites as untrusted ❺. Options ❻ lets you configure the program, add sites to a whitelist ❼ and block or allow embedded items ❽.

4 Open Options in Firefox and click the Privacy tab ❶. By default, Firefox will remember your browsing history ❷, but you can clear recent data ❸ and delete individual cookies ❹. You can choose the time range to clear ❺ and click the Details button ❻ to select items to remove ❼.

5 Private Browsing mode stops Firefox remembering and storing details of any sites you visit. You can turn every browsing session into the equivalent of a private one by selecting 'Never remember history' in the drop-down box ❶. You may also want to 'clear all current history' ❷ as well.

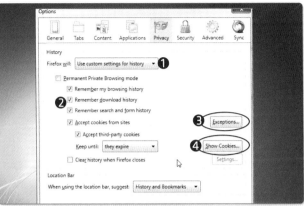

6 You can use the custom settings ❶ to allow only certain sites in your browser history ❷. You can manage cookies from here as well. Prevent the browser accepting cookies from certain sites by clicking Exceptions ❸. Show Cookies ❹ will let you see what's currently stored on your computer.

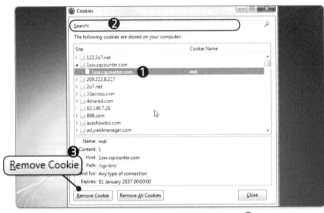

7 You can browse the complete list of cookies ❶ or filter it by typing a word or a few characters into the Search box ❷. Expand a folder and click on a cookie to see some information about it. If it's not from a site you recognise, select the folder and click Remove Cookie ❸.

8 Firefox can automatically clear your personal details every time you close it. Tick the 'Clear history when Firefox closes' box ❶ and click the Settings button next to it ❷ to select the items to remove ❸. Certain things such as passwords and site data should be left alone.

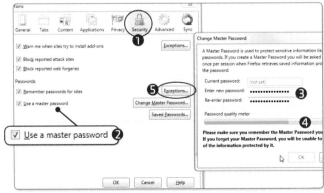

9 Click the Security tab ❶ and tick the option to use a master password ❷. Enter a secret word or phrase ❸ and the 'password quality meter' ❹ will show you how strong it is. You can also tell Firefox not to remember passwords for certain sites. Click Exceptions ❺ and then enter the addresses.

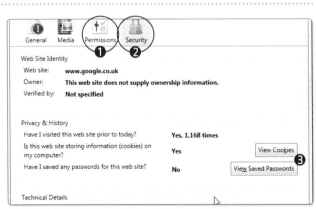

10 Control what a website is allowed to do – load images, share your location and so on – by right-clicking the page and selecting View Page Info. Go to the Permissions tab ❶ to change settings. Click the Security tab ❷ to see saved cookies and passwords for that site ❸.

Surf anonymously using a proxy server

http://walln.com ⏱ 5 mins

One of the simplest ways to remain anonymous online and reduce the risk of identity theft is to use a proxy server. Proxies, which are perfectly safe and legal, act as a buffer between you and the web. They hide your IP address so you can visit sites without revealing your identity or location.

1 Visit Proxy 4 Free (http://bit.ly/proxy262) for a list of proxy servers you can use. It gives each server a rating based on speed, reliability and how long it's been active. You can also see where each server is based. We're choosing the highly rated German web-based proxy Walln (www.walln.com) **1**.

2 Before you enter the address of the site you want to visit, press 'options' **1**. By default, Walln encodes the URL of sites **2** and allows cookies **3** – we recommend you leave these settings as they are. The other boxes – to remove objects **4**, encode pages **5** and remove scripts **6** – are optional.

3 Tick Remove Objects to decrease page-loading time by removing Flash and Java objects. Encoding pages and removing scripts adds extra layers of security, but might stop some sites working properly. Once you've decided on your settings, enter the site's address **1** and press Go **2**.

4 As you continue browsing, you can change the options in the bar at the top **1**. You also have the option of clearing cookies here **2**, so if you're visiting a site that doesn't need them and you don't want your activity tracked, you can click on this option.

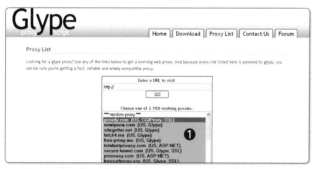

5 For another list of proxy servers, visit Glype (www.glype.com), a web-based proxy script that many of the Proxy 4 Free sites use. When we visited, it listed nearly 3,000 servers **1**, all of which are powered by Glype's script.

6 Proxify (https://proxify.com) has similar options to Walln, but offers different configurations that have been specially built for speed, security and compatibility **1**. Tick the options you want **2**, enter the URL **3** and hit Proxify **4**.

Encrypt your entire PC

www.truecrypt.org ⏱ 10 mins

Even if your PC is password-protected, it doesn't necessarily make it secure. TrueCrypt is a free and easy way to encrypt files, USB drives or even your whole computer to keep it completely private and safe. It runs on Windows 7, Vista and XP, Mac OS X and Linux.

1 When you start encrypting something with the software, TrueCrypt creates a new 'volume' in which to store your files, which is like a hidden area on your disk. To open the encryption wizard, click Create Volume ❶.

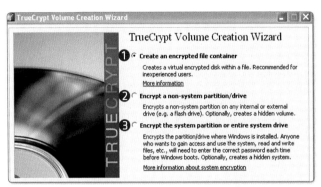

2 Choose 'Create an encrypted file container' ❶ to encrypt files and folders, 'Encrypt a non-system partition/drive' ❷ for external disks and USB drives or 'Encrypt the system partition or entire system drive' ❸ for your entire PC.

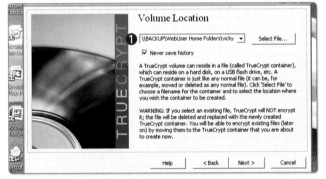

3 For file encryption, select 'Standard TrueCrypt Volume', give it a name and choose where you want to save it ❶. The size of the volume should be based on what you want to keep in it. External disk sizes are set automatically.

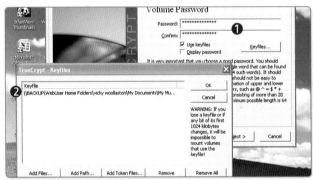

4 Choose a password ❶. To make it extra secure, add an optional keyfile ❷. This is any file that can be used like a physical key to unlock the encryption. Format the volume on the next screen to save it.

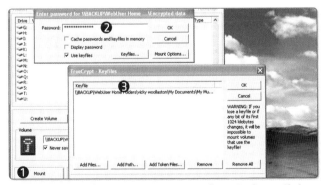

5 Mount the volume to access it in Windows Explorer. Click Select File, find the volume, select a drive letter and press Mount ❶. Enter the password ❷ and attach any keyfiles ❸. Auto-Mount Devices is for USB drives. Double-click the entry to open it like a normal disk. To re-encrypt, click Dismount.

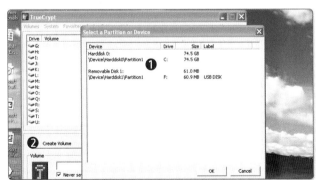

6 To encrypt a partition, external disk or USB drive, plug it in and click Select Device. Choose the drive ❶ and launch the wizard by clicking Create Volume ❷. Encrypting drives wipes them of their content, so back up any files and then drop them back into the volume once they've been mounted.

WEBSITE-BUILDING WORKSHOPS

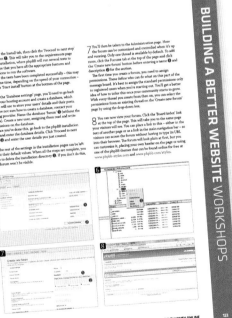

p122

Add panoramic images

www.adobe.com/uk ⏱ **1 hour 30 mins**

A panorama can place a building in context within its landscape, or be used to show an entire room in one shot. You don't need special equipment – just a steady hand, a digital camera and a photo-editing package. Here we're using Adobe Photoshop CS2 to create a panorama automatically, but you can use any photo editor that supports layers to do it manually.

1 You'll need to take several shots of your subject. It's best to use a tripod, so all the shots line up perfectly. If you don't have a tripod you can do it freehand, but make sure you place the camera on a static object such as a table or a wall when you take the shots.

You can minimise the visibility of the join between images by locking the exposure settings and white balance on your camera; refer to your manual if you're not sure whether this is possible on your camera. This will help to eliminate contrast variations between photos.

2 Open Adobe Photoshop and select File, Automate, Photomerge. Select the files you want to include, click OK ❶ and Photoshop will attempt to stitch them together. You may find that some photos can't be processed. These will remain in the bar at the top of the page ❷.

3 If Photoshop has managed to merge all your photos and the seams aren't overly visible, you can crop the image into a rectangle ❶ and then save it, ready for use. However, if any images haven't been added to the panorama, they can be dragged from the top toolbar and placed in position manually. Try to line up the images as closely as possible, and Photoshop will snap them into place. If a seam is noticeable, try dragging one of the images slightly and attempting the join again.

4 You can include the panorama as a normal image on your website. However, the MapLib tool gives visitors the chance to scroll around and zoom in or out ❶ of the image. Register for a free account at www.maplib.net and click My Pictures to upload your image. The viewer is based on code from Google Maps. Click the Share tab to see the code, and cut and paste it where you want the image to appear on your website.

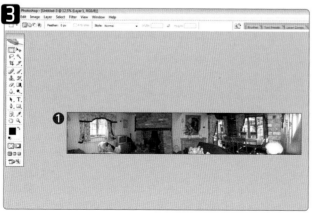

Add driving directions

http://bit.ly/drivegadget ⏱ **30 mins**

If visitors to your website need to know how to get somewhere, you can easily provide the tools necessary to show them the way. Rather than including a map of the local area as a static JPEG image, you can add Google Maps' Driving Directions gadget, making it easier for your visitors to find their way.

1 Visit http://bit.ly/drivegadget and click the 'Add to your webpage' button ❶ to load the configuration page.

2 First, change the default Location ❶ to the country in which you will be requiring directions. You should also change the Language in the drop-down box ❷ to your preferred language. In our example, the gadget will be used only to direct people to a fictitious holiday cottage called Redcot Barn, so the most important detail for us to include is the address, and this goes in the End Address box ❸. A nice touch is to add a helpful message to the Start Address box ❹ so, for example, you could type 'Enter your postcode, eg DA4 2HW'.

3 The last step in customising the gadget is to change the colour and size of the box. If you're placing the gadget in a sidebar, you can tailor it to fit perfectly by editing its width and height ❶. If the gadget is the focus of a page, you can leave the width at its default value, but it's worth increasing the height from 91 to 100 pixels to avoid the clutter of a vertical scrollbar.

Next, choose a border for the box ❷. You can add a title ❸ for the gadget, or leave the box empty if you don't need one. At any point, you can click the Preview Changes button ❹ to see how your options will look. Once you've customised everything, click the 'Get the Code' button ❺ to reveal the code in the text box below.

4 Cut and paste this code into the page where you want the gadget to appear, and save the file. The resulting directions appear in a new browser window, since this gadget redirects visitors to Google Maps.

1

2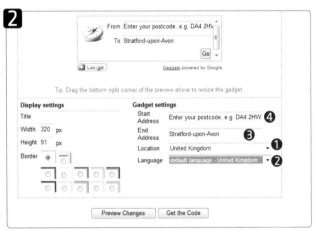

3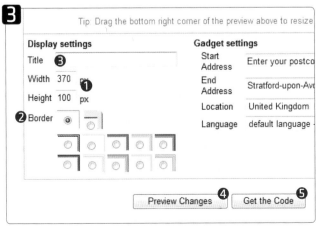

4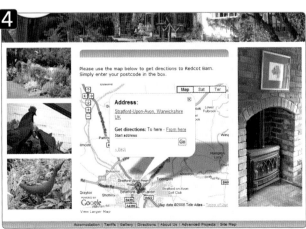

Add photo slideshows

http://picasa.google.com ⏱ **1 hour**

Sometimes you'll want to show visitors to your site more than just a couple of photos, and that's when a slideshow works wonders. Here's how to create a simple slideshow using Google's free photo-organising application, Picasa.

1 To create an online gallery, you'll need a Google account. Visit the Picasa website and create a new account, or log in if you already have one. Accept the Terms and Conditions and click the Free Download button ❶ if you haven't already installed Picasa.

2 In Picasa, create a new album by clicking the Upload button. Add a title and any other details you want, and choose the Public or Unlisted option. On the next page, you'll be prompted to install the Picasa Uploader. Once this is installed, choose the photos to upload. Next, click on the album's page and make a note of the RSS feed address by right-clicking the RSS link at the bottom of the page and choosing Copy Shortcut ❶.

3 Go to http://bit.ly/picasagadget and click the 'Add to your webpage' button to see the Preferences page. Paste the feed you copied in Step 2 into the Picasa Web RSS Feed box ❶ on the Preferences page. Remove the text from the title box ❷ and increase the size of the gadget so the image can be seen without cropping ❸. View the effect of any changes made by clicking Preview Changes.

4 Once you're happy with how it looks, click the 'Get the Code' button and copy and paste the code into your web page where you want the slideshow to appear. If you update the images in the Picasa Web Album, the new images will appear on your website automatically.

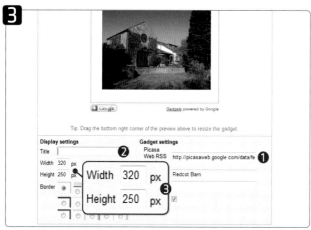

Add an MP3 player

www.google.com   ⏱ **20 minutes**

If you're a musician, a website is a great way to draw attention to your work, and it's easy to add a gadget enabling visitors to listen to your efforts.

For most musicians seeking to give their profiles a boost, a page at MySpace (www.myspace.com) will suffice. However, if you want something bespoke, a Google gadget will enable visitors to stream songs directly from your site.

Many sites play a MIDI file automatically when they load, but don't be tempted to do this on your site. The poor-quality files sound old-fashioned, and it's bad etiquette to play a song without first asking the visitor.

1 Upload an MP3 file to your web host using an FTP client, or via your site's Control Panel. This will be the file streamed every time a user clicks the Play button. For this reason, you should lower the quality of the file (by reducing its bit rate in an audio convertor) to speed up loading times and ensure you don't use up lots of bandwidth.

Once the file has been uploaded to your web host, you will need to make a note of its URL.

2 This free player provides a Play/Pause button ❶ and a progress bar ❷, allowing a track to be played directly from your site. Go to http://tinyurl.com/mp3gadget. Click the 'Add to your webpage' button ❸ to get to the Preferences page.

3 Here you need to insert the URL for the file you wish to play on your site ❶. Also, remove the text in the Title box ❷; you're better off adding a title in your web page. Edit the height of the gadget to 55 pixels ❸ to remove the vertical scroll bar. Then change the colour of the border ❹ to match the colour scheme of your website.

4 Once you've finished editing the preferences of the gadget, click the 'Get the Code' button and copy the code displayed in the text box. You'll need to paste this into your web page, wherever you want the MP3 player to appear.

Once you've saved the HTML file, the media player should appear and work as you'd expect.

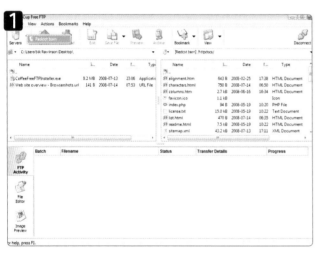

Add internet forums

www.phpbb.com 🕑 **30 minutes**

Having a regular group of visitors to your site is great, but giving them a way to converse makes them stay on your site for longer, potentially earning you more advertising revenue, and it adds value for users who share a common interest. For example, if your website is for a local mums' and toddlers' club, a forum offers a way for members to chat to each other, arrange meetings, swap tips and offer advice.

It's sensible practice to make people sign up with an email address and password to prevent spam posts. To prevent libellous or nasty posts, you must also moderate the forum, or delegate the job to someone you trust.

In this walkthrough, we'll show you how to get a forum up and running using phpBB, a popular open-source forum program. You'll also need a web-hosting account with a MySQL database and PHP support.

1 See if your web host has an automatic installation service. Sometimes phpBB can be installed at the click of a button using a tool called Fantastico; look for it in your hosting provider's control panel. If you find it, use this install method and go to Step 7. If not, download the latest version of phpBB and extract the files to a folder on your desktop.

2 Next, upload the files to a new folder on your web server using your FTP software. If you don't have FTP access, upload the single zipped file using your host's file manager and then unzip the file from the online control panel.

3 Once the files have been uploaded to your web server, you need to configure the installation. To do this, open your web browser and enter the address of your forum. This will be your domain name, followed by the name of the folder containing the phpBB files. You will then be taken to the main installation page for phpBB.

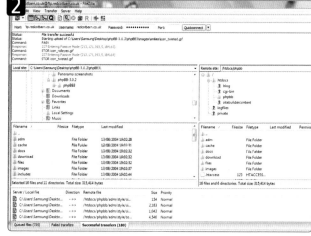

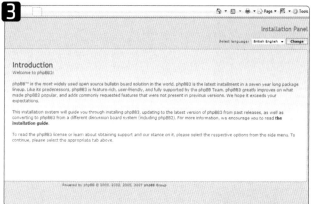

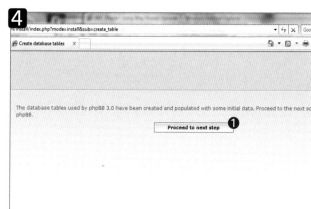

4 Click the Install tab, then click the 'Proceed to next step' button ❶. This will take you to the requirements page for the installation, where phpBB will run several tests to make sure that you have all the appropriate features and permissions to run the software.

Once the tests have been completed successfully – this may take some time, depending on the speed of your connection – click the 'Start install' button at the bottom of the page.

5 On the 'Database settings' page, you'll need to go back to your hosting account and create a database, which phpBB will use to store your users' details and their posts. If you're not sure how to create a database, contact your hosting provider. Name the database 'forum' ❶ (without the quotes). Create a new user, assigning them read and write permissions on the database.

Once you've done this, go back to the phpBB installation page and enter the database details. Click 'Proceed to next step' ❷ and enter the user details you just created.

6 The rest of the settings in the installation pages can be left at their default values. When all the steps are complete, you have to delete the installation directory ❶. If you don't do this, the forum won't be visible.

7 You'll then be taken to the Administration page. Here the forum can be customised and controlled when it's up and running. Only one thread is available by default. To add more, click the Forums tab at the top of the page and click the 'Create new forum' button before entering a name ❶ and description ❷ for the section.

The first time you create a forum, you need to assign permissions. These define who can do what on this part of the message board. It's best to assign the standard permissions only to registered users when you're starting out. You'll get a better idea of how to tailor this once your community starts to grow. With every thread you create from then on, you can select the permissions from an existing thread on the 'Create new forum' page by using the drop-down box.

8 You can now view your forum. Click the 'Board index' link at the top of the page. This will take you to the same page your visitors will see. You can place a link to this – either in the text of another page or as a link in the main navigation bar – so visitors can access the forum without having to type its URL into their browser. The forum will look plain at first, but you can customise it, placing your own header on the page or using one of the phpBB themes that can be found online for free at www.phpbb-styles.com and www.phpbb.com/styles.

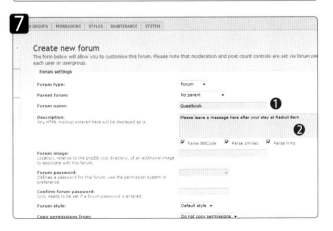

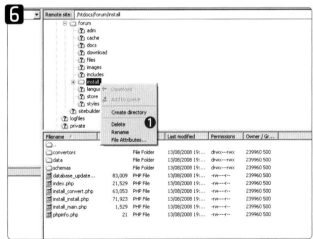

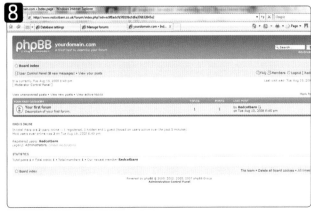

Add YouTube videos

www.youtube.com ⏱ **30 minutes**

J ust a few years ago, hosting a video on a website was a complicated matter. Thankfully, this has changed. Adding a video clip to your site can be done in a few minutes, and all for free. Here we show you how to add a YouTube video to your site.

1 Prepare your video for uploading. YouTube accepts videos in a range of formats, including AVI, MPG and MOV. For the best results, use an MPEG4 format such as DivX or XviD. A free video encoder such as Any Video Converter (www.any-video-converter.com) will change your video to one of these formats. Select 640x480 as the resolution ❶ – this will give the best quality because of the way YouTube compresses files. Clips can't be longer than 10 minutes, and are limited to 1GB in size.

2 To upload your clip, you need a YouTube account. If you don't have one, sign up for free at www.youtube.com. Once you're registered, click the Upload link at the top of the screen, then click the yellow 'Upload video' button ❶ and browse for your file in the window that appears. Uploading takes a while,

since your broadband connection's upload speed is likely to be much slower than the download speed. For this reason, we recommend limiting your video's file size to around 20MB.

3 Once your video is uploaded, YouTube processes it. We now have to embed it into our website. Even before the processing is done, you'll see a message saying that the upload is complete. Below it, you'll see a box containing some code ❶. Copy and paste this code into the web page on which you want the video to appear.

4 Visitors to your website can now see the video when they look at your website. They simply have to click the large play button overlaid on the video ❶ to view it.

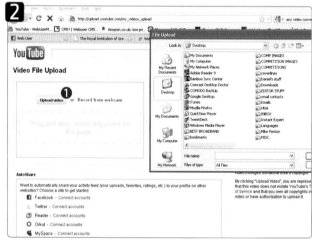

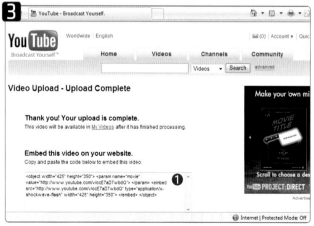

Turn your ideas into cash

EMAIL WORKSHOPS

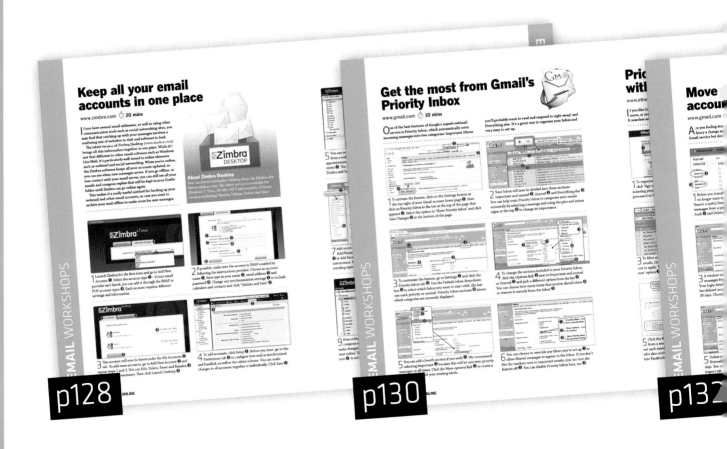

Get the most from
Windows Live Mail 2011

http://explore.live.com/windows-live-mail

Manage your email

Windows Live Mail lets you access multiple POP and IMAP accounts from one location. Here's how to use it

Keep all your email accounts in one place

www.zimbra.com ⏱ **20 mins**

If you have several email addresses, as well as using other communication tools such as social-networking sites, you may find that catching up with your messages involves a confusing mix of websites to visit and software to load.

The latest version of Zimbra Desktop (www.zimbra.com) brings all this information together in one place. While it's not that different to other email software such as Windows Live Mail, it's particularly well-tuned to online elements such as webmail and social networking. When you're online, the Zimbra software keeps all your accounts updated, so you can see when new messages arrive. If you go offline, or lose contact with your email server, you can still see all your emails and compose replies that will be kept in your Drafts folder until Zimbra can go online again.

This makes it a really useful method for backing up your webmail and other email accounts, in case you want to archive your mail offline to make room for new messages.

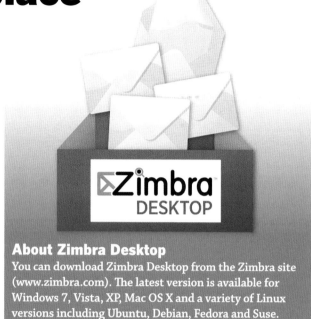

About Zimbra Desktop
You can download Zimbra Desktop from the Zimbra site (www.zimbra.com). The latest version is available for Windows 7, Vista, XP, Mac OS X and a variety of Linux versions including Ubuntu, Debian, Fedora and Suse.

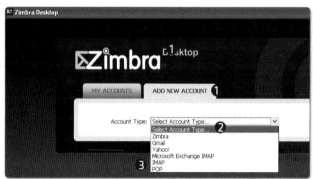

1 Launch Zimbra for the first time and go to Add New Account ❶. Select the account type ❷ – if your email provider isn't listed, you can add it through the IMAP or POP account types ❸. Each account requires different settings and information.

2 If possible, make sure the account is IMAP-enabled by following the instructions provided. Choose an account name ❶, then type in your name ❷, email address ❸ and password ❹. Change any synchronisation settings ❺ to include calendars and contacts and click 'Validate and Save' ❻.

3 This account will now be listed under the My Accounts ❶ tab. To add more accounts, go to Add New Account ❷ and repeat steps 1 and 2. You can Edit, Delete, Reset and Reindex ❸ any accounts if necessary. Then click Launch Desktop ❹.

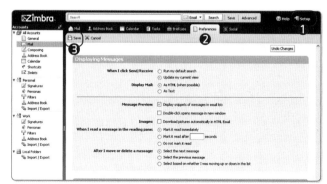

4 To add accounts, click Setup ❶. Before you start, go to the Preferences tab ❷ to configure how mail is synchronised and handled, as well as the colour scheme. You can make changes to all accounts together or individually. Click Save ❸.

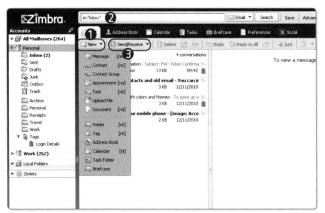

5 You can email directly from Zimbra, even emailing offline from a webmail address. Create new emails, contacts, appointments, tasks and folders from the New drop-down menu ❶. The search box ❷ searches all files and folders within Zimbra and Send/Receive ❸ manually syncs everything.

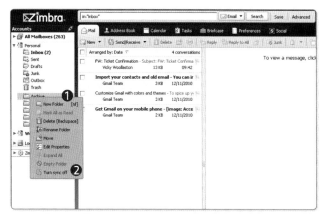

6 To clear mailbox space in your email inbox, you can archive your emails in Zimbra. Create a folder from the New menu. Right-click it ❶ and select 'Turn sync off' ❷. Files will only be stored locally. Repeat and select 'Turn sync on' to undo this.

7 Add social-networking accounts in the Social tab ❶. Click Add/Remove Accounts ❷ and choose Add Twitter Account ❸ or Add Facebook Account ❹ and follow the onscreen instructions. Move feeds by clicking the arrows ❺ and view trending topics and Digg categories on the sidebar ❻.

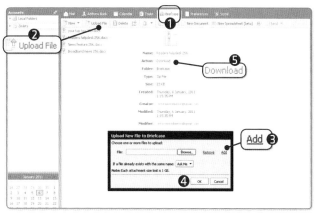

8 You can store and create documents in the Briefcase tab ❶. Click Upload File ❷ and select the files you want – you can add more than one at a time. Click Add ❸ then OK ❹. The files will be stored online as Zip files and can be downloaded ❺ when needed.

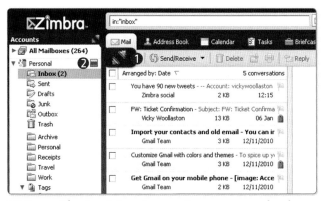

9 Even without an internet connection, you can read and compose emails – even webmail, if you've synced it – and make changes to documents. Changes will update when you're next online. You can activate offline working by clicking the icon ❶. A red square ❷ shows which accounts are offline.

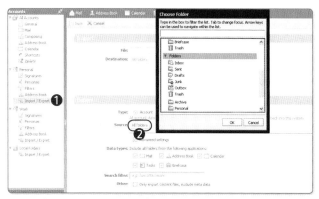

10 If you want to create a backup of your files, folders or entire Zimbra accounts, select the Preferences tab and click Import/Export ❶ on the account you want to back up. Under Export, select All folders ❷. This will open a pop-up box so you can choose which files to back up.

Get the most from Gmail's Priority Inbox

www.gmail.com ⏱ 10 mins

One of the best features of Google's superb webmail service is Priority Inbox, which automatically sorts incoming messages into two categories: Important (those you'll probably want to read and respond to right away) and Everything else. It's a great way to organise your Inbox and very easy to set up.

1 To activate the feature, click on the Settings button at the top right of your Gmail account home page ❶, then click on Priority Inbox in the bar at the top of the page that appears ❷. Select the option to 'Show Priority Inbox' and click Save Changes ❸ at the bottom of the page.

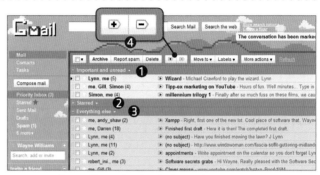

2 Your Inbox will now be divided into three sections: Important and unread ❶, Starred ❷ and Everything else ❸. You can help train Priority Inbox to categorise your emails accurately by selecting a message and using the plus and minus signs at the top ❹ to change its importance.

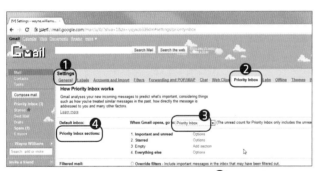

3 To customise the feature, go to Settings ❶ and click the Priority Inbox tab ❷. Use the Default inbox drop-down box ❸ to select which Inbox you want to start with: the last one used, priority or normal. Priority Inbox sections ❹ shows which categories are currently displayed.

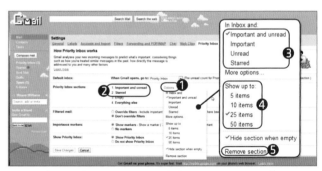

4 To change the sections included in your Priority Inbox, click the Options link ❶ next to Important and unread or Starred ❷ and pick a different option from the list ❸. You can choose how many items that section should show ❹ or remove it entirely from the Inbox ❺.

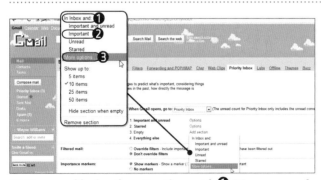

5 You can add a fourth section if you wish ❶. We recommend selecting Important ❷ because this will let you view priority messages at all times. Click the More options link ❸ to create a section from any of your existing labels.

6 You can choose to override any filters you've set up ❶ to allow filtered messages to appear in the Inbox. If you don't like the markers next to important emails, you can turn the feature off ❷. You can disable Priority Inbox here, too ❸.

Prioritise your messages with OtherInbox

www.otherinbox.com ⏱ 10 mins

If you like Gmail's Priority Inbox but wish it would do more, or you use Yahoo Mail, OtherInbox is for you. It searches and sorts any commercial messages into relevant folders as they arrive, whether they're from Amazon, Facebook or Skype. To turn it off, log into the website, scroll down to the bottom and click Disconnect.

1 To organise a Gmail inbox, type in your email address and click 'Sign up'. Enter your password and the service will begin scanning your messages. You can see how many emails it's processed so far ❶ and how many you can organise ❷.

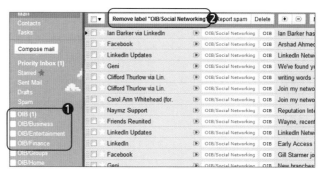

2 When the scanning process has finished, it will create a bunch of new OIB labels ❶. Click any of these to view the messages it contains. If an email is incorrectly labelled, select it and click 'Remove label' ❷.

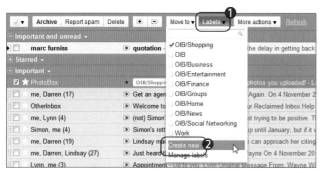

3 To filter messages from other senders, select one of their emails, click the Labels button ❶ and choose the relevant one to apply. To create additional OIB labels, click the 'Create new' option ❷ and then name it – OIB Photobox, for example.

4 Go to https://my.otherinbox.com and log in. If there are any senders you don't want organising, untick them ❶. You can rename a sender by clicking on its entry ❷. The drop-down box ❸ will let you choose a different label or create a new one.

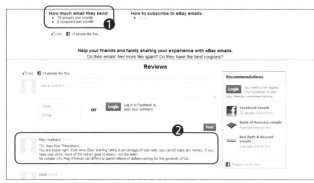

5 Click the Review link to rate and review communications from a sender. It will tell you how many emails they send out each month ❶, and you can read comments from people who also receive those messages ❷. You'll need to be logged into Facebook to post your opinion.

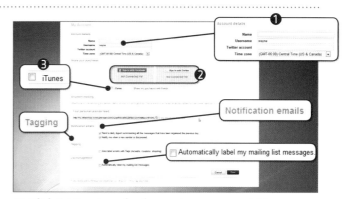

6 Click Settings to make changes to your account. You can alter your details ❶, connect to Facebook and Twitter ❷ and share iTunes purchases with friends ❸. You can also turn off the daily notification emails ❹, allow tagging ❺ and label messages received via a mailing list ❻.

Move your Hotmail account to Gmail

www.gmail.com ⏱ 10 mins

Are you feeling stuck with your Hotmail account? If you fancy a change and want to switch to Google's popular Gmail service but don't want to lose all your messages and contacts, there's a simple and tidy solution: just export your existing data to a Gmail account. You can also switch from a Yahoo, AOL or other webmail account.

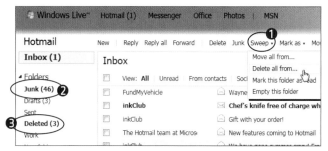

1 Before you transfer your messages to Gmail, delete any you no longer want to keep, such as old newsletters and offers. There's a useful Sweep function ❶ that will let you delete all messages from a particular sender. Be sure to empty your Junk ❷ and Deleted folders ❸ too.

2 To move your remaining messages to Gmail, open a new account and then go to Settings ❶. Click the 'Accounts and Import' tab ❷. This lets you transfer emails from a range of popular services, including Hotmail, Yahoo and AOL. Click on the 'Import mail and contacts' button ❸.

3 A window will open, asking where you want to import your messages from. Enter your Hotmail address and password. Your login details are held by TrueSwitch (Google's partner), but deleted according to your preference after a maximum of 30 days. Choose what to import from the list ❶.

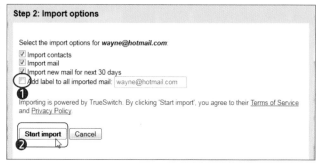

4 By default, imported messages will be labelled with your old email address, so you can see where they've come from. If you don't want this to happen, untick the option ❶ to label imported mail. Click Start import ❷ and Gmail will go to work. This process can take several hours.

5 Unless you unticked the option, TrueSwitch will copy new Hotmail messages to your Gmail account for the next 30 days. You can extend this period by going to the Accounts and Import tab on the Settings page and clicking Add POP3 email account ❶. Enter your Hotmail address in the box ❷.

6 In the next box that opens, enter your Hotmail password ❶. The server and port details will be filled in automatically. Tick the option to Leave a copy of the retrieved messages on the server ❷ if you want the emails to remain available through Hotmail, and click on Add Account ❸.

Keep your email free from spam

www.mailwasher.net ⏱ 20 mins

Some webmail services have impressive spam filters, but email software such as Outlook Express or Windows Live Mail, which uses an address from your ISP or your own domain name, could leave you overwhelmed with unwanted junk emails. MailWasher is a free program that filters your mail before the spam gets to your inbox.

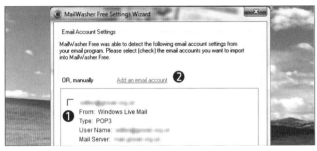

1 Once installed, you'll be prompted to use the wizard to set up your email. If you already have your email set up in Windows Live Mail or something similar, it should find your existing details ❶. Select the account, click Next and skip to Step 3. Otherwise, select the 'Add an email account' link ❷.

2 Work through the tabs at the top. On Mail Account ❶ give the email account a name ❷ and enter the address ❸. Incoming Mail ❹ is for entering the POP3 or IMAP details, and 'Bouncing and Outgoing Mail' ❺ is for the SMTP settings. You can get these from your email provider's support pages.

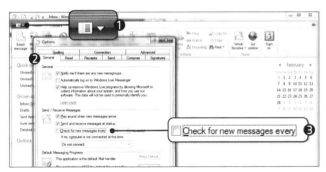

3 Ensure that automatic downloading of mail is turned off in your email software – Windows Washer will forward messages on to it once it's done. In Windows Live Mail, click the File menu ❶ and select Options, then Mail. On the General tab ❷ deselect the 'Check for new messages every' option ❸.

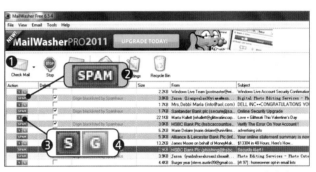

4 Back in MailWasher, select your email software and click Finished. Click the Check Mail button ❶ to download your messages. Any spam that MailWasher finds will be marked with a Spam icon ❷, but many messages will be unknown and labelled with both S (for spam) ❸ and G (for good) ❹.

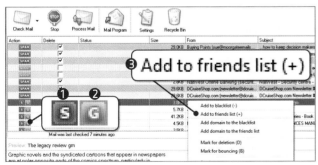

5 You can help MailWasher learn what's spam and what's not by clicking the S button ❶ on spam messages and the G button ❷ on good messages. Find a message from someone you know, right-click on their email message and select 'Add to friends list (+)' ❸.

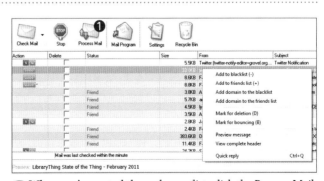

6 When you've sorted through your list, click the Process Mail button ❶. This will strip out the confirmed spam and send the remaining messages to your email software. You should regularly check your MailWasher software to keep teaching it what's safe to send straight through to your inbox.

Get the most from
Windows Live Mail 2011

http://explore.live.com/windows-live-mail

The latest version of Windows Live Mail has had a major makeover, gaining the ribbon interface found in most modern Microsoft programs. This puts all the important features and commands within easy reach, while tucking away lesser functions (such as folder management and views) in relevant tabs along the top of the screen.

To install the Windows Live Mail software, you'll need to run the Windows Live Essentials downloader, choose the custom option and pick Mail from the list of available programs. You can also install other Windows Live applications, such as Messenger, Photo Gallery and Movie Maker, at the same time if you wish.

Manage your email

Windows Live Mail lets you access multiple POP and IMAP accounts from one location. Here's how to use it

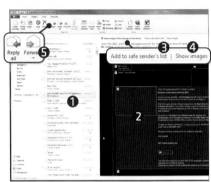

1 Adding accounts to Live Mail couldn't be simpler. Enter an email address ❶ and password ❷ and choose a display name for sent messages ❸. The software will recognise Hotmail and Gmail addresses, and fill in the settings automatically. You can manually configure the server settings for other email accounts ❹.

2 The message headers will be displayed in a strip on the left ❶, with the contents shown in the reading window on the right ❷. If the message contains images you'll either need to add the sender to your safe list ❸ or click the 'Show images' link ❹ to view them. Reply to a message or forward it using the buttons in the ribbon ❺.

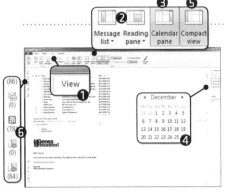

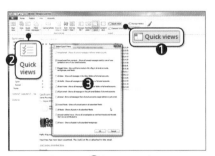

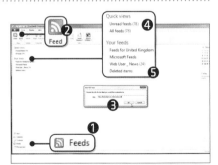

3 The default layout is designed for widescreen monitors, but you can change it by clicking View ❶. Click Message list or Reading pane ❷ and select the option you want. Calendar pane ❸ toggles the calendar ❹ on or off, and Compact view ❺ reduces the width of the panel on the left ❻.

4 Quick views ❶ lets you filter your inbox to show just unread messages, emails from contacts or unread feeds. You can turn the Quick Views feature on or off ❷ and also add or remove filters by clicking the 'Quick views' button and selecting the ones you want ❸. Click OK to update the views list.

5 To set up and view web feeds, click the Feeds option ❶, followed by the Feed button ❷. Then enter the URL of the site you wish to subscribe to ❸. The list of feeds will appear on the left and you'll be able to view all unread stories ❹ or browse the subscriptions individually ❺.

QUICK ACCESS TOOLBAR
The most commonly used options can be accessed through the title bar menu. Click the down-arrow to choose which ones to display.

JUNK
Select a message and click this button to mark it as spam and remove it from your inbox. Click the down arrow to access the safety options.

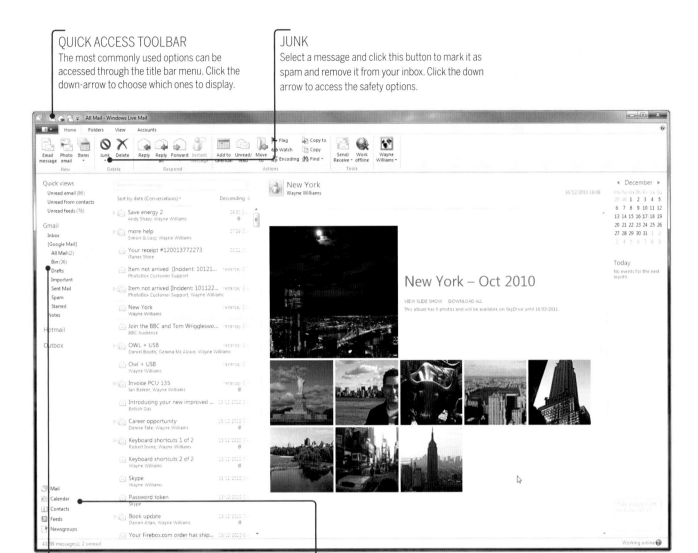

FOLDERS
It's easy to organise your inbox: just create some folders and drag messages to them.

CALENDAR
Clicking this button will open the Calendar full screen. You can add events by right-clicking a date or by using the 'Add to calendar' button on the Home tab.

6 You can send high-resolution photos to friends without overloading their inbox by using Windows Live SkyDrive as a holding area. Click the 'Photo email' button ❶ and then sign in to Windows Live Mail using your Live ID ❷. If you don't have one, click the link to sign up for a new account ❸.

7 Browse for the photos you want to add to the new message. The photos will be laid out in an album view ❶. You can edit the text ❷, change the layout design and turn the expiration date option on or off ❸. When a friend receives the email they'll be able to view the photos by clicking the thumbnails.

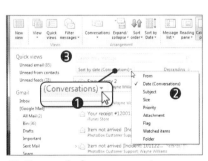

8 You can find any message in your inbox by sorting or searching for it. Click the Sort by arrow ❶ and choose the criteria you want to use to order your inbox ❷. If you've picked a different view you can click the column header. Alternatively, type a sender name or message text into the search box ❸.

MUSIC & VIDEO WORKSHOPS

Upgrade your videos to HD

www.adobe.com/uk/products/premiereel 5 mins

I f you've been making home video for any length of time, the chances are you've got hours of footage tucked away on tapes or your hard disk. The trouble is, it may be in 4:3 format rather than widescreen, and will almost certainly lack the definition of the HD footage you can get from relatively cheap cameras today. However, with a few simple tweaks you can update old video footage for the modern era. While you're not going to get HD quality out of lower-quality footage magically, you can go some way to boosting the picture and the resolution to give more of an HD impression.

The downside is that you'll have to buy some digital video software to do the job. There are plenty of options, but we've plumped for Adobe Premiere Elements 9, which has all the tools you'll need. Free video-editing options are fairly thin on the ground, but there are tools you can use in Windows Live Movie Maker to boost the appearance of standard-definition video for playing on HD screens (http://explore. live.com/windows-live-movie-maker).

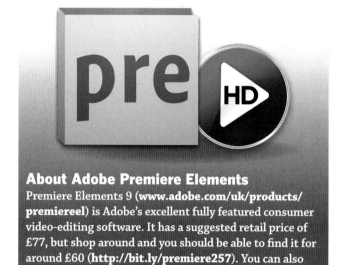

About Adobe Premiere Elements

Premiere Elements 9 (**www.adobe.com/uk/products/ premiereel**) is Adobe's excellent fully featured consumer video-editing software. It has a suggested retail price of £77, but shop around and you should be able to find it for around £60 (**http://bit.ly/premiere257**). You can also buy it in a bundle with Adobe Photoshop Elements 9.

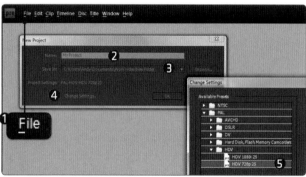

1 From the File menu ❶ choose New, Project (or select 'new project' from the intro screen). Give the project a name ❷ and choose where to save it ❸. Click on the Change Settings button ❹ and select HDV 720p 25 ❺.

2 Import the file you want to edit by selecting the Organize tab ❶. Click Get Media ❷, then Files and Folders ❸ and choose the file you want to upscale. If you want to use more than one video and edit them together, load all the videos now.

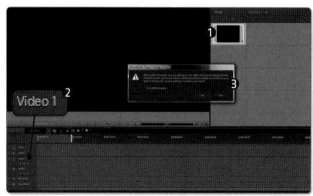

3 Click and hold your video ❶ and drag it down to the timeline bar towards the bottom of the screen. Drop it into the slot labelled Video 1 ❷. You may get a warning that your formats are mismatched. Click No ❸ because you want to upgrade your video.

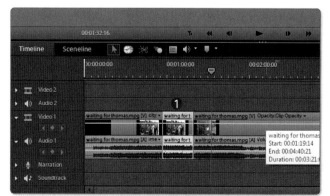

4 If you want to edit your video before upgrading it, now is a good time to do it. To cut sections from your video, go to the beginning of the section to cut and press Ctrl+K. Do the same at the end of the section you want to cut. Make sure the section is highlighted ❶, then press Delete.

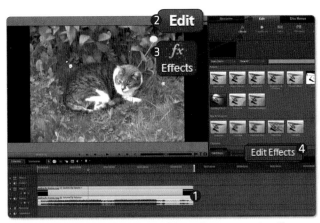

5 If your video was shot on an older video camera, it will probably be in 4:3 ratio, while your new project will be 16:9 widescreen. To change it, make sure your whole timeline is selected ❶ and click the Edit tab ❷ and Effects ❸. Then click the Edit Effects button ❹.

6 Click the arrow next to Motion ❶ and make sure the Uniform Scale box ❷ is ticked. Drag the scale slider ❸ to the right until the picture fills the screen. You'll want a bit of overlap in order to ensure that no black lines appear on the final video.

7 This may harshly crop sections of video. Select a scene you want to adjust, making it into a clip using Ctrl+K if necessary. Hover your mouse over the vertical position ❶ until the cursor turns to an arrow. Click and drag the number to adjust the position up and down, and click Done ❷.

8 A couple of other features can also improve the appearance of your video. If it's blurry, click Sharpen ❶ then Apply ❷. Modern cameras use image stabilisers to eliminate camera shake, but if your video is a little shaky, you can add this retrospectively with the Image Stabilizer option.

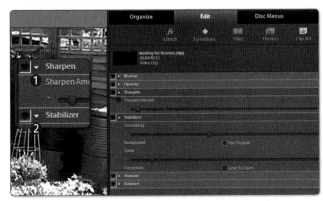

9 Click Edit Effects again. Click the arrows next to Sharpen ❶ and Stabilizer ❷ to adjust the settings. Increase the Sharpen Amount very slightly, but don't go over the top or it will be too much. Check the Stabilizer options; the default settings should be OK.

10 Click the Share tab ❶. You can either choose to write the file to Blu-ray or DVD from the Disc option, or alternatively, to save an HD file, click Computer. Choose MPEG, click the down arrow next to Presets and select 'HD 720p 25'. Name the file and save it.

Create a Google Earth video tour

www.google.com/earth ⏱ 20 mins

Google's virtual globe software lets you do all sorts of cool things, from exploring shipwrecks to getting up-to-date weather forecasts.

One of our favourite features is the ability to create and share video tours. If you've been on holiday, for example, you can use the software to relive your adventures, flying from location to location, and returning to all the sights you saw along the way. You can add descriptions for each place, complete with links and photos, and even record a narration to go with it – a bit like a director's commentary. Recorded tours can be saved in Google Earth, exported to your hard disk, emailed and shared online.

Tours don't just have to cover holidays – they can be about anything that interests you, from the wonders of the world to famous World War Two battle sites. For inspiration, click the Earth Gallery button in the Layers panel and browse the collection of tours and places that have been created and shared by other Google Earth users. Hover your mouse over a thumbnail to find out more about it, then click View Now to open it in the software.

About Google Earth

Available for Windows, Linux and Mac OS X, Google Earth can be downloaded for free from **www.google.com/earth**. The latest version introduces several new features, including real-time weather tracking, presenting data collected from GPS devices and an integrated web browser.

1 To create a tour, fly to the starting point and zoom in until you're at the right position. Click the Add Placemark icon ❶. A yellow pushpin will appear ❷ – click and drag this into place. You can also manually adjust the Latitude and Longitude co-ordinates ❸. Give the location a name ❹.

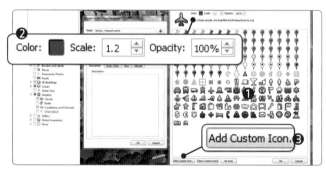

2 You can change the pushpin placement icon to something else by clicking it and selecting one of the alternative choices ❶. You can alter its colour, scale and opacity, too ❷. Google Earth also lets you use custom icons. Just click the button ❸ and browse for a suitable image file.

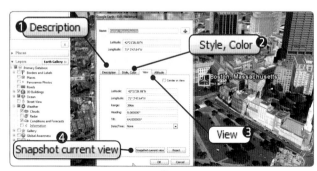

3 You can enter a description ❶ for the location, use HTML and add links. Style, Color ❷ changes the colour, size and opacity of the label and icon. You can fine-tune the placemark's default 3D position, including its range, heading and tilt, under View ❸. Click 'Snapshot current view' ❹ to save it.

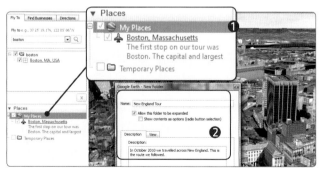

4 Click OK and the first stop on your tour will be added to the My Places panel ❶. If you need to make changes, right-click the entry and select Properties. It's worth creating a folder for all the placemarks. Right-click My Places and select Add, Folder. Give it a name and description ❷.

5 Drag the first place into your new folder ❶. Fly to your next destination, create a placemark for it and save it to the folder. Repeat the process for your other stops. When you've finished, click on the folder. You'll see a little Play Tour icon at the bottom of the panel ❷. Click this to begin your tour.

6 Google Earth will now fly you from location to location, pausing briefly at each placemark along the way. A set of controls at the bottom left will let you pause, resume, rewind and fast-forward through the locations ❶. You can also loop the tour. The controls will fade out of view when not in use.

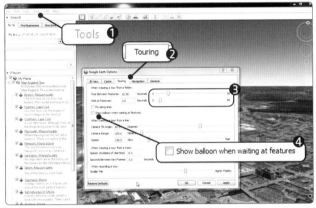

7 You can adjust the speed of the tour by going to Tools ❶, then Options, and clicking the Touring tab ❷. Use the sliders ❸ to change the length of time between features and the wait at each one. You can have Google Earth display a balloon showing information about each stop ❹.

8 Click the camera icon ❶. This will open the recording tools. Zoom out of Google Earth to the 'world view', then click the Record button ❷ to record your tour. Explore the first location, rotating around interesting buildings, then click the next stop in your folder to fly there.

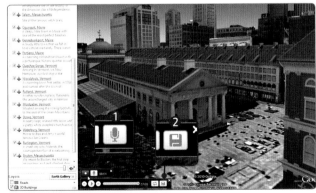

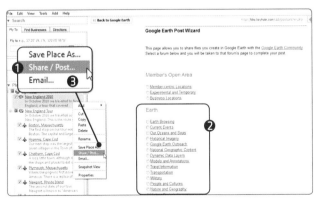

9 The Audio button ❶ lets you add optional narration. When you've finished recording your tour, click the Record button again and Google Earth will play it back. If you're happy with the results, click the Save icon ❷ and give the tour a name and description. It will appear in the My Places panel.

10 To share your tour, right-click on it. Share/Post ❶ will let you upload it to one of the Google Earth Community forums ❷. Just select the board you want, sign up or log in, and complete the post. Email ❸ will let you send the tour as a KMZ attachment via Gmail or your default email program.

☑ **YES!** Please start my subscription to *Web User* with **3 issues for just £1.** After 3 issues I understand that my subscription will continue by Direct Debit at the **LOW RATE of just £19.99 every 13 issues – saving 23%** on the cover price – unless I write to cancel within my introductory period. If I do cancel, no further money will be taken from my account. The **3 issues for £1** are mine to keep, whatever I decide

Step 1: Complete your details below

Mr/Mrs/Ms

First name

Surname

Job title

Company

Address

Postcode

Daytime tel

Mobile tel

Email

Year of birth (YYYY)

Cheque or Credit/Debit Card

1 I enclose a cheque made payable to *Dennis Publishing Ltd.*

2 Credit/Debit card: Please charge my:

☐ VISA ☐ MasterCard ☐ AMEX ☐ Debit/Maestro (Issue No. ☐)

Card No.

Start date (if applicable)   Expiry date

Signed   Date

Step 2:

3 Direct Debit Payment – Just **£1 for 3 issues,** then £19.99 every issue (UK only).

Dennis **Instruction to your Bank or Building Society to pay by Direct Debit** ● **DIRECT Debit**

Please complete and send to: Freepost RLZS-ETGT-BCZR, Dennis Publishing Ltd, 800 Guillat Ave, Kent Science Park, Sittingbourne ME9 8GU
Name and full postal address of your Bank or Building Society

To the manager: Bank name

Address

Postcode

Account in the name(s) of

Branch sort code

Bank/Building Society account number

Originator's Identification Number

| 7 | 2 | 4 | 6 | 8 | 0 |

Ref no. to be completed by Dennis Publishing

Instructions to your bank or Building Society
Please pay Dennis Publishing Ltd. Direct Debits from the account detailed in this instruction subject to the safeguards assured by the Direct Debit Guarantee. I understand that this instruction may remain with Dennis Publishing Ltd and, if so, details will be passed electronically to my Bank/Building Society.

Signature(s)

Date

Banks and building societies may not accept Direct Debit instructions for some types of account

Now return your completed form to:
Freepost RLZS-ETGT-BCZR,
Web User Subscriptions,
800 Guillat Ave, Kent Science Park,
Sittingbourne ME9 8GU

(No stamp required)

Offer code: P1009MB

YOUR GREAT DEAL

★ **3 issues for JUST £1**

★ Pay nothing more if you decide *Web User* isn't for you

★ **FREE delivery** direct to your door

Subscription Offer

3 issues of Web User
FOR JUST £1

Web User, the UK's favourite internet magazine, is bursting with practical advice to help you get the best out of the web and your PC.

Claim **3 issues for £1** today and get *Web User* delivered free to your door every fortnight.

Inside every issue of Web User you'll find:

▶▶ **Websites** – We bring you the best new and revamped websites on the internet

▶▶ **Software** – We review all the latest software. Plus, we tell you about top free software you can download online

▶▶ **PC & web tips** – We reveal fantastic tips to help you improve your PC and use the internet better

CALL NOW:
0844 322 1289

Visit **www.dennismags.co.uk/webuser**

using the offer code: P1009MB

Make a screencast video with Expression Encoder

http://bit.ly/practical253 🕙 **15 mins**

There are all sorts of reasons why you might want to record your on-screen activity: to show someone how to use a program or a website, for example, or to capture streaming content from a live broadcast. The best-known tool for the job is Camtasia (www.techsmith.com/camtasia). It's an excellent product that does everything you could want, but it's expensive: the Windows version costs £231.

Microsoft's Expression Encoder is a great free alternative. Its main purpose is to enable developers to generate high-quality video content for the web using Silverlight, but it comes with a built-in screen-capture tool that can record high-definition videos, with or without narration. Individual recordings are limited to a maximum of 10 minutes, but most screencasts are nowhere near that long, and you can record as many as you like. Recordings can be saved in Windows Media format, so anyone can view them.

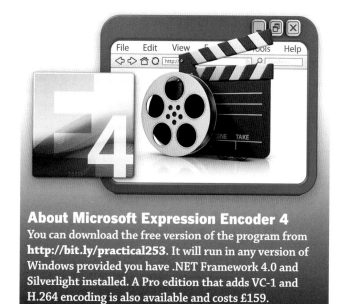

About Microsoft Expression Encoder 4
You can download the free version of the program from **http://bit.ly/practical253**. It will run in any version of Windows provided you have .NET Framework 4.0 and Silverlight installed. A Pro edition that adds VC-1 and H.264 encoding is also available and costs £159.

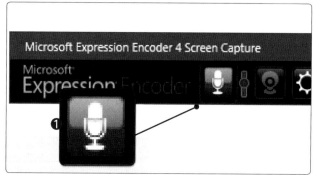

1 Run the Expression Encoder 4 Screen Capture tool from the Start menu. The utility is a small floating bar with five icons. To add narration to your screencast, click the Audio button ❶ and adjust the volume using the slider.

2 Click the webcam icon ❶ to enable a picture-in-picture view. Hover your mouse over it and you'll see a live feed from your camera ❷. You won't see the webcam image during capture – it only appears when you edit the recording in Expression Encoder.

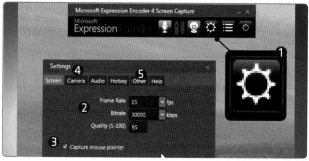

3 Click the Edit Options button ❶ to open the Settings box. You can change the frame rate, bitrate and quality ❷ here, and set the program to capture the mouse pointer ❸. If you've enabled your webcam, click Camera ❹ to change the settings. You'll find some useful extra options under Other ❺.

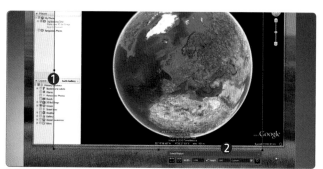

4 Once you've got everything set up, click the red Record button. The toolbar will vanish temporarily and be replaced by a crosshair. Click and drag to select the area to capture. This will be outlined with a resizable red border ❶. When you let go of the mouse, the Select Region box ❷ will open.

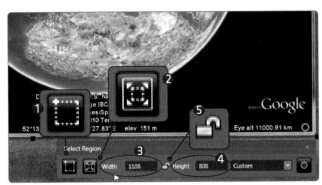

5 The Define Capture Area button ❶ lets you redraw a new area, while the Resize Windows button ❷ will change the dimensions of the window you're recording so it fits neatly inside the capture area. You can manually adjust the width ❸ and height ❹ if necessary. The padlock ❺ will lock the ratio.

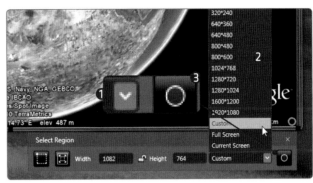

6 If you want your screencast to be a particular size, click the Preset arrow ❶ to show a selection of choices ❷. You may need to click the Resize Windows button afterwards so the application will match the new dimensions. When you're ready, click Record ❸. A three-second countdown will appear.

7 As soon as the countdown ends, recording begins. The red border is replaced by flashing green corners ❶. Everything you do inside the selected area is recorded. The box outside the window ❷ shows the size and frame details. You can pause and stop recording, and hide the controls.

8 When you click Stop, recording will stop and the saved file will appear in the Capture Manager. To watch it back, click the Play button on the left. A new video preview window will open ❶. You can pause and play the capture ❷ and toggle between full-screen and window modes ❸.

9 If you're not happy with your capture, you can delete it ❶ and start again. You can also change the output folder here for any future recordings ❷. Clicking 'Send to Encoder' ❸ will open the main Expression Encoder program and load the capture, ready for editing and saving.

10 You can position the webcam overlay ❶ anywhere, or remove it entirely. Use the controls ❷ to watch your screencast and make edits, such as trimming any boring bits. You can change the Output format and the video and audio codecs ❸. Click Encode ❹ to save the finished recording.

Share and stream audio over a network

iTunes & Windows Media Player ⏱ 5 mins

Most people store their digital music on one computer. This is fine if you only ever listen to your music on that computer, but what if you want to enjoy your songs on another PC elsewhere in the house? One solution is to copy your tracks and playlists to the other computer, but then you'll end up with duplicate copies of the same files on different hard disks – an unnecessary waste of disk space if you have a home network.

A better approach is to stream the music over your home network. This is easy to set up and can be done using iTunes or Windows Media Player. You'll need to install the same program on every computer you want to listen to your music on. The setup process for streaming music using iTunes is explained first, followed by the process for Windows Media Player 11 and 12, starting at Step 6.

About iTunes & Windows Media Player
Both iTunes and Windows Media Player (WMP) are free to download. Apple iTunes is available for Windows and Mac from **www.apple.com/itunes/download**. There are 32- and 64-bit versions available. WMP 11 is included with Vista and can be downloaded for XP from **http://bit. ly/wmp250**. Version 12 is available only with Windows 7.

1 iTunes: The Home Sharing feature streams music around networked computers and lets you copy tracks between them. Click Home Sharing ❶ and log in to your iTunes account ❷. If Home Sharing isn't listed, select Turn On Home Sharing from the Advanced menu ❸. Click the Create Home Share button ❹.

2 Now launch iTunes on your second computer and log in to Home Sharing as you did in Step 1. Click on the Home Sharing option ❶ on the sidebar and you'll be able to browse or play your songs as if there were stored locally. You'll also be able to copy tracks from your other PC's library to this computer's local library by dragging and dropping them.

3 If you only want to play songs, not copy them, go to Edit, Preferences and click the Sharing tab ❶. Tick the 'Share my library on my local network' box ❷. Decide if you want to share your entire library or just selected playlists ❸. You can also protect the shared content with a password ❹.

4 Anyone connected to your network will now be able to listen to your music, provided they also have a copy of iTunes installed. Run the program on the computer that you want to stream the music to, then go to Edit, Preferences. Click the Sharing tab and tick 'Look for shared libraries' ❶.

5 iTunes will now search your network and display any available collections under Shared in the sidebar **1**. Browse the list of playlists and songs just as you would a local library, select some music and click Play to begin streaming it. It should start playing after a few seconds.

6 **Windows Media Player:** To share music using WMP 11, click the arrow under Library **1** and select Media Sharing. You can find songs over the network and share your own **2**. Click Networking **3** to open the Windows Network and Sharing Center. Now launch WMP on the other PC.

7 To share libraries in Windows 7 using WMP 12, click the arrow next to Stream **1** and select 'Automatically allow devices to play my media'. In the box that opens, click 'Automatically allow all computers and media devices' **2**. The box will close and your content will now be available.

8 You don't need to be running the same version of Media Player to stream files. The newly shared collection should appear under Other Libraries **1**. Just click the type of media you want to access. You can browse music files by artist, album and genre. Double-click a song to play it.

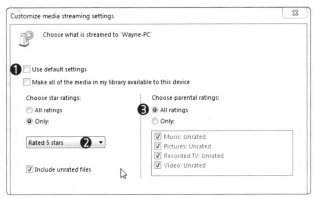

9 Click the arrow next to Stream and select 'More streaming options'. Here you can rename your media library **1**, use the drop-down box to show devices on the local or all networks **2** and block or customise access to certain computers **3**. You can also remove unwanted devices.

10 Select the option to customise a computer's settings and you'll be able to stop younger users from streaming music or movies aimed at older audiences. Untick 'Use default settings' **1** and choose the star **2** and parental **3** ratings instead.

Find free MP3s as you browse the web

http://ex.fm ⏱ 10 mins

Exfm (http://ex.fm) is a Google Chrome extension that looks for MP3 files on websites as you browse the internet. When it finds tracks available to download for free, it adds them to a library so you can play, pause and queue them. You can then access songs stored in your library at any time.

1 Install the add-on and start browsing. When Exfm finds a site offering free music, it will automatically import the songs into its library. The button next to the Search bar ❶ will show you how many tracks have been found and added. Click the button to view them ❷.

2 You can play or queue all the songs in the list ❶ or play them individually ❷ by selecting the track in the library. An extended player will be added to the bottom of the screen ❸ to control your music while you browse the site. Click the Home button ❹ to open the library.

3 The library shows all the tracks added so far. Double-click on one to start listening to it. You can also right-click on a song to play or queue it ❶. If you've accumulated a lot of music, the Search box ❷ will help you find the tracks you want.

4 Click the Pane View button ❶ to switch to an alternative layout. This lets you view songs by site ❷, artist ❸ or album ❹. You can see how many times you've listened to a particular track ❺ and if it's failed to load ❻.

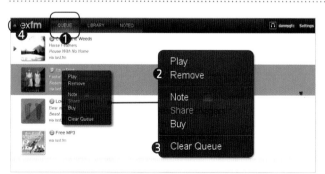

5 Click the Queue button ❶ to access the saved playlist. Right-clicking on a song will let you play or remove it ❷ and you can also clear the queue ❸. The small Home icon next to the exfm logo ❹ at the top of the page will take you to the Exfm website.

6 Right-click on the Exfm button and select Options. When you sign up for an account ❶ you'll be able to sync your library across multiple computers, as well as connect to Facebook ❷ and Twitter ❸. You can also enable notifications and keyboard shortcuts from here.

MUSIC & VIDEO WORKSHOPS

Convert video files and share them online

www.freemake.com/free_video_converter ⏱ **10 mins**

Digital videos come in a wide range of different formats. If a movie is in one format and you need it in another to watch it on a particular player or phone or to send it to the web, for example, you'll need some conversion software. Free Video Converter is simple-to-use software that converts video to any format, and it's free to download.

1 If you're planning to share your video online, enter your account details to make the process faster. You can store account details for YouTube, Facebook and Nicovideo. Go to File ❶, Options, then the Accounts tab ❷ and enter your details ❸. You can clear saved data with the dustbin icon ❹.

2 Add media from your computer or from other devices by going to the File menu ❶ and choosing Add Video, or by using the +Video button ❷. Browse to the file ❸ on your hard disk and open it. Only supported files are displayed, and you can add multiple files in one go.

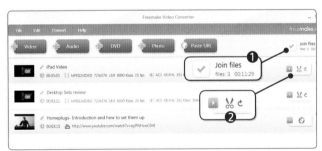

3 To link multiple files so they're converted into a single video, select the ones you want to merge and tick 'Join files' ❶. To make basic edits to your video and audio, click the scissor icon ❷ on the relevant file and a new window will open.

4 Once uploaded, choose how to convert your files using the options at the bottom ❶. Each will automatically reformat the media to the required size and dimension ❷. You can see the full list of supported files and formats in File, Options.

5 To upload your videos to your YouTube account, select the file to send and click the 'to YouTube' button ❶. If you saved your login details in Step 1, the file will automatically begin uploading ❷. If it didn't save your details, a window will appear for you to enter them.

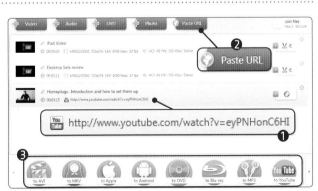

6 To convert YouTube videos to DVD or for playing on another device, copy the video link ❶ and click Paste URL ❷. This will add the video to the list. Choose which format to convert it to from the menu below ❸. You'll need a DVD writer installed to create a DVD.

PROBLEM-SOLVING WORKSHOPS

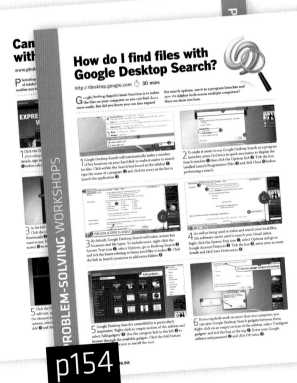

files

P

About Windows Live Mesh 2011

p158

How can I check my hard disk's health?

http://gsmartcontrol.berlios.de ⏱ 20 mins

Hard-disk failure can be catastrophic. However, all hard disks come with a built-in feature called S.M.A.R.T. (Self-Monitoring, Analysis and Reporting Technology),

which can be used by compatible software to spot any potential problem. Here we explain how to use the free GSmartControl tool to keep an eye on your hard disk's health.

PROBLEM-SOLVING WORKSHOPS

How do I solve Windows 7 problems?

Windows 7 Troubleshooting ⏱ 5 mins

If you've upgraded to Windows 7 but are having problems with your computer, you may be able to get the operating system to fix itself. Troubleshooting is a new option in

Windows 7's Control Panel that can analyse your PC for a variety of common problems, suggest fixes and even carry them out for you.

PROBLEM-SOLVING WORKSHOPS

How can I add photos to Google Earth?

Picasa, Picasa Web and Google Earth ⏱ 20 mins

C an you remember exactly where all your photos were taken? Geolocating your pictures when you get back from a trip adds a new dimension to viewing and sharing them later. Once they have a location added to them, you can even view them in Google Earth.

1 Open Picasa (http://picasa.google.com) and choose the photos, folder or album ❶. Click the Places button ❷ to open the Places sidebar ❸. Search for a location ❹ or change the map type ❺ and scroll around it to pinpoint the exact position.

2 Click the green map marker button ❶ and click again where you want the photos to be located. You can drag the marker around the map. When you're happy, click OK ❷ in the 'Place photos here' box. Repeat for all the photos you want to locate.

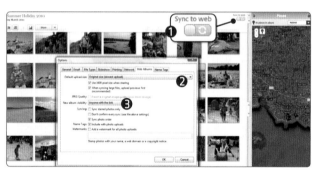

3 Make sure all your geolocated photos are selected and flick the 'Sync to web' switch ❶. You'll need to sign into your Google account if you haven't done so already. Click Change Settings to choose your upload options, such as size ❷ and privacy settings ❸. When you're done, click OK.

4 Go to your Picasa Web Albums page (http://picasaweb. google.com) and click on the album you just uploaded. You should see your photos and a map of their location ❶. Click an individual photo to fine-tune its placement. Under the map, click 'Edit location' ❷ and move the marker on the map ❸.

5 You can also 'Upload to Panoramio' if you'd like your pictures to appear when people browse the area on Google Earth. Return to the Album view and click the 'View in Google Earth' (http://earth.google.co.uk) link ❶. Save the file to which it links somewhere safe ❷.

6 From Google Earth's File menu ❶, choose Open and load the file. The map will zoom to a view that covers all your photos. To turn everyone else's photos off, untick Photos under Layers ❷. Your photos are listed in Temporary Places ❸. To make them permanent, drag them into My Places ❹.

Can I edit photos online without installing software?

www.photoshop.com/tools 🕙 30 mins

Photoshop Express Editor is a free, cut-down version of Adobe's powerful image-editing application. It enables you to edit your images online, without downloading or installing any software, so you can use it on any computer. Here, we take a look at what this surprisingly powerful free tool has to offer.

1 Click the Create Account link at the top of the www.photoshop.com/tools page. After filling in all the requested details, sign into your account and click the Online Tools menu **1** before selecting the Photoshop Express Editor option **2**.

2 Click the Upload Photo button. Use the browser window to select an image on your hard disk and click Open. Your image will open in the online editor **1**. To increase your workspace, click the 'Toggle full-screen mode' button **2**.

3 In the left-hand pane is a selection of editing tools **1**. Click the one you'd like to use to display a series of preview thumbnails **2**. Click the one that represents the setting you want to use. You can use the Undo option at the bottom of the screen **3** to reverse any unwanted changes.

4 Additional options are available in the Advanced section of the left-hand pane **1**. Here you can apply special effects and filters in the same way as the other tools. Changes and effects can be reversed by clearing the tick box next to an item **2** and reapplied by ticking it.

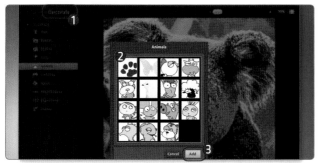

5 Click the Decorate link at the top of the left-hand pane **1** to add text, symbols and other graphics to your image. Select the element you would like to add from the list of available options, select a specific element in the pop-up window **2**, click Add **3** and then resize and position as required.

6 When you're happy with your image, click Done, choose the size you'd like to use and click Save **1**. The image can be saved to your hard disk. To make it available online, select the Photoshop Express Organizer option from the start screen and upload it to your library.

How do I find files with Google Desktop Search?

http://desktop.google.com 🕐 **30 mins**

Google Desktop Search's basic function is to index the files on your computer so you can find them more easily. But did you know you can also expand the search options, use it as a program launcher and sync its sidebar tools across multiple computers? Here we show you how.

1 Google Desktop Search will automatically index a number of key locations on your hard disk to make it easier to search for files. Click within the Search box found in the sidebar ❶, type the name of a program ❷ and click its entry in the list to launch the application ❸.

2 To make it easier to use Google Desktop Search as a program launcher, press Ctrl twice in quick succession to display the Search window ❶ then click the Options link ❷. Tick the box labelled Launch Programmes/Files ❸ and click Close ❹ before performing a search.

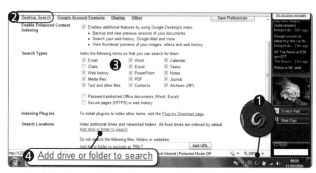

3 By default, Google Desktop Search will index certain key locations and file types. To include more, right-click the System Tray icon ❶, select Options, go to Desktop Search ❷ and tick the boxes relating to items you'd like to index ❸. Click the link in Search Locations to add extra folders ❹.

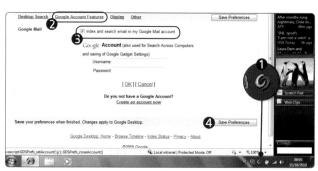

4 As well as being used to index and search your local files, the software can be used to search your Gmail inbox. Right-click the System Tray icon ❶, select Options and go to Google Account Features ❷. Tick the box ❸, enter your account details and click Save Preferences ❹.

5 Google Desktop Search's extendibility is particularly impressive. Right-click an empty section of the sidebar and select 'Add gadgets' ❶. Use the category link to the left ❷ to browse through the available gadgets. Click the Add button beneath a gadget's icon to install the tool.

6 If you regularly work on more than one computer, you can sync Google Desktop Search gadgets between them. Right-click on an empty section of the sidebar, select 'Configure gadgets' and tick the box at the top ❶. Enter your Google address and password ❷ and click OK twice ❸.

Can I browse my favourite websites offline?

www.httrack.com ⏱ 20 mins

Despite the advent of Wi-Fi and mobile broadband, there are times when going online isn't an option. Fortunately, it's possible to download sites for offline browsing using HTTrack (www.httrack.com), which grabs a site's content and structure so you can browse it just as you would online.

1 HTTrack is very easy to use. The interface looks like a version of Windows Explorer, with the local drives arranged on the left ❶. Click the Next button, then give your new project a name ❷ and a category ❸. Choose where you want to save sites ❹ and then click Next.

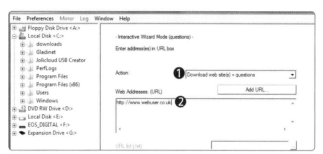

2 Choose an action in the drop-down box ❶. By default, this is 'Download web site(s)' but there are other options, such as 'Test links in pages (bookmark test)'. It's worth selecting 'Download web site(s) + questions' and using the interactive mode. Enter the web address of the site you want to grab ❷.

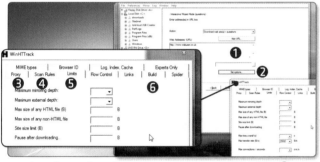

3 If you have a list of URLs in a text file, you can add it ❶. Click 'Set options' ❷ and move through the tabs to set up everything how you want. You can configure a proxy ❸, use wildcards to exclude or include links under Scan Rules ❹, set grabbing limits ❺ and set how links are saved in Build ❻.

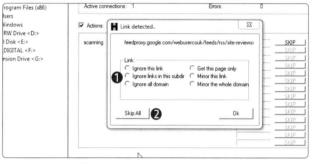

4 Click Next, change the final connection parameters if necessary, and click Finish. The program will begin to grab pages. In interactive mode, it asks what to do with an external link. Select an option in the box ❶ or choose Skip All ❷ to have the question dealt with automatically.

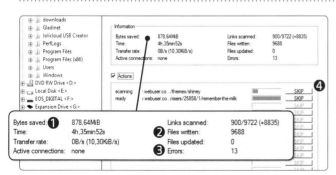

5 The parsing process can take several hours depending on the size of the site, so leave it running in the background. The Information box will show how much has been saved so far ❶, the number of files written ❷ and any errors ❸. It will also show what it's currently doing and let you skip an action ❹.

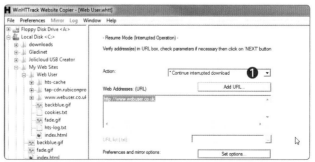

6 If you lose your connection, you can resume downloading later. From the main screen, click Next, select the project in the drop-down menu, click Next again, then 'Continue interrupted download' ❶. When it's done, double-click the file in the Save directory to open the stored site in your browser.

How do I sync the files on different PCs?

http://explore.live.com/windows-live-mesh ⏱ **20 mins**

M any of us use more than one computer, whether it's at work, school or on a network at home. But how many times have you found yourself sitting at one computer, wishing you had access to the files stored on another?

The old-fashioned solution to this dilemma has been around since the days of the floppy disk – save your files and take them with you. While modern USB memory drives bring this up to date, you still have to remember to save your changes, and your data is always at risk of getting stolen or lost. Even emailing files to yourself isn't foolproof – you might simply forget to do it.

Microsoft's Windows Live Mesh 2011 takes all the hassle out of this process. This file-syncing software automatically keeps your files and folders synchronised across any Windows 7 or Vista PC. As an added bonus, you can also configure it to sync up to 5GB of files to SkyDrive, Microsoft's free online storage space.

About Windows Live Mesh 2011

Windows Live Mesh 2011 runs on Windows 7 and Vista. It comes as part of the Windows Live Essentials package, but you can choose not to install any of the other software elements. You'll need a Windows Live account or Hotmail address, and the software must be installed on each computer you want to sync.

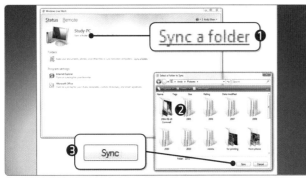

1 To make sure that files in a particular folder are kept up to date on all your PCs, click 'Sync a folder' ❶. Browse to a folder you want to sync ❷, select it and click the Sync button at the bottom ❸.

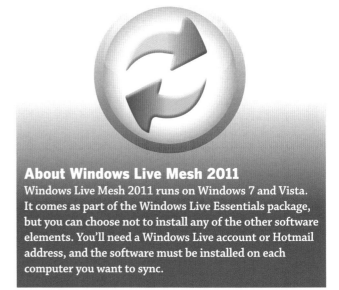

2 You need to select where you want the file synced. Choose one or more of the other computers ❶ on which you've installed the software. You can also choose to store the folder online at SkyDrive ❷ – see Step 7.

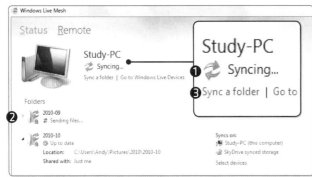

3 The software will start synchronising the files on all your devices ❶. You can monitor its progress in the Folders section ❷, and add more folders to synchronise by clicking 'Sync a folder' ❸ again.

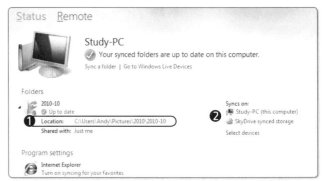

4 Click a folder to see further options. Clicking the Location ❶ will take you directly to the folder. You can add new files to the folder or delete files from it. These changes will be copied across to the other devices that share that folder ❷.

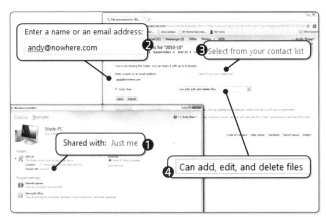

5 Click the 'Just me' link ❶ and a browser window will open. You may be required to sign in. You can then add up to nine people to share the folder with by entering their email address ❷ or choosing from your Hotmail contacts ❸. Once chosen, select what the person can do with the folder ❹.

6 Click on one of the computers to access the configuration options. You will be shown the folders synced to that computer. Click Personalize ❶ to change the computer's nickname (this doesn't affect its network name) and icon. Manage ❷ lets you turn syncing off.

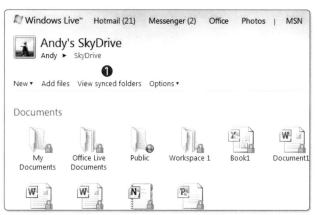

7 You can also sync your files with SkyDrive. Up to 5GB of your free 25GB of SkyDrive storage can be used for syncing. Highlight a folder you want to sync ❶, click 'Select devices' ❷, put a tick in the box next to 'SkyDrive synced storage' ❸ and finally click OK ❹.

8 If you're using a computer that doesn't have Windows Live Mesh installed on it, you can still access folders you've synced with SkyDrive. Open your web browser, go to http://skydrive.live.com and log in with your details. You can then click the 'View synced folders' link ❶ to access your files.

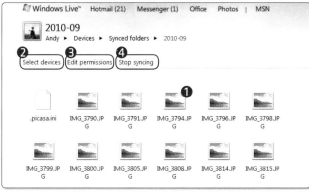

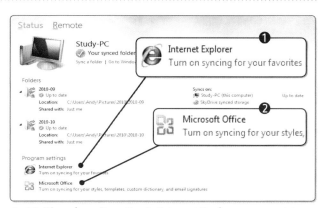

9 Clicking a folder takes you to the files stored within it. Click a file's icon ❶ to download it. 'Select devices' ❷ lets you choose the computers to which the folder is synced. 'Edit permissions' ❸ invites others to share the files, and 'Stop syncing' ❹ will remove it from SkyDrive.

10 If you have Favorites in Internet Explorer you want to sync across the browsers on your linked computers, click 'Turn on syncing for your favorites' ❶. You can also do this with Microsoft Office settings ❷ to synchronise templates, the custom dictionary, styles and email signatures.

How can I check my hard disk's health?

http://gsmartcontrol.berlios.de 🕐 **20 mins**

Hard-disk failure can be catastrophic. However, all hard disks come with a built-in feature called S.M.A.R.T. (Self-Monitoring, Analysis and Reporting Technology),

which can be used by compatible software to spot any potential problems. Here we explain how to use the free GSmartControl tool to keep an eye on your hard disk's health.

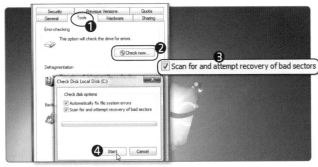

1 Windows comes with its own disk-checking tool. Open Explorer, right-click the disk you want to examine and choose Properties. Select the Tools tab ❶ and click the 'Check now' button ❷ under 'Error-checking'. Tick 'Scan for and attempt recovery of bad sectors' ❸ and click Start ❹.

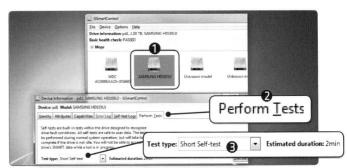

2 GSmartControl (free from http://gsmartcontrol.berlios. de) can also test a disk for errors. Run the program and double-click the disk icon ❶ to open a new window containing information about your hardware. For now, just click the Perform Tests tab ❷ and select a test to run ❸.

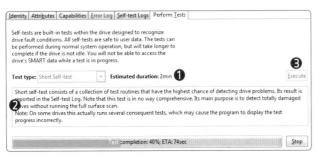

3 GSmartControl offers three types of scan: short, extended and conveyance. You can see how long each test is likely to take ❶ and find out more about it ❷. Begin with a short test, and run an extended one if problems are detected. Click Execute ❸ to begin.

4 When the test finishes, it will hopefully have done so without finding any errors. Click the 'Self-test Logs' tab ❶ to view the results. The Error Log tab ❷ lists five of the most recently reported problems. Click View Output ❸ to get a breakdown of the test results and any potential problems.

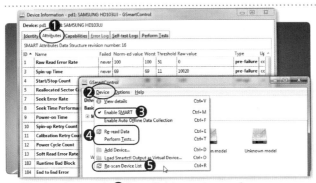

5 The Attributes tab ❶ lists all drive actions and any problems. Hover your mouse over an item in the list to view an explanation. The Device menu ❷ lets you toggle S.M.A.R.T. on or off ❸, re-read data and perform tests ❹ and scan the device list again ❺.

6 Unusual sounds emanating from your hard disk can be a sign of impending failure. You can find a collection of these sounds and their possible causes at the DataCent website (http://bit.ly/workshop1250). Locate your disk manufacturer and click the Play button ❶ to hear an example and compare it to your disk.

How do I solve Windows 7 problems?

Windows 7 Troubleshooting ⏱ 5 mins

If you've upgraded to Windows 7 but are having problems with your computer, you may be able to get the operating system to fix itself. Troubleshooting is a new option in Windows 7's Control Panel that can analyse your PC for a variety of common problems, suggest fixes and even carry them out for you.

1 Select Control Panel from the Start menu, type Troubleshooting into the search boxand click the main Troubleshooting heading when it appears. If this is the first time you've used it, click Yes ❶ for the most up-to-date content.

2 Click an area you're having problems with from the list on the main page. To see all the tools available, click View all. Look for an option that matches your problem; for example, the troubleshooter can look at Internet Explorer's performance ❶.

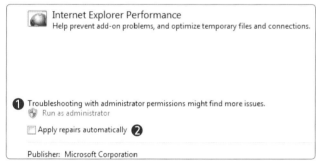

3 Click the Advanced link, then 'Run as administrator' ❶ to find extra problems. You may need to type in your administrator password if you're not already in an administrator account. Untick 'Apply repairs automatically' ❷ if you'd rather see what's going on. Click Next.

4 The software will search for any problems, then report on what those potential issues may be ❶. If you want the software to fix the problem, leave a tick in the box. Click 'View detailed information' ❷ to show the problems the software looked for but didn't find.

5 Click Next and you may be offered more options ❶, particularly if you're being asked to disable something. With the Internet Explorer performance example in step 2, you may decide to keep some add-ons, while others can be removed ❷. The effect on performance is also shown ❸.

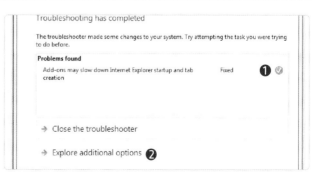

6 When the fixes have been made, the troubleshooter will report on its performance ❶. If it hasn't been able to solve the problem, try clicking 'Explore additional options' ❷. This will offer a range of extra things you can try to fix the problem, such as online help and system recovery.

How do I merge the best bits from photos?

Windows Live Photo Gallery 2011 and Paint.net ⏱ **20 mins**

Taking photos of a group of people is tricky; there always seems to be someone who's blinking, grimacing or somehow spoiling the picture.

However, if you take a stream of photos, you can use the Photo Fuse facility in Windows Live Photo Gallery 2011 to merge the best bits.

1 Launch Windows Live Photo Gallery 2011 (http://bit.ly/ wlpg263 – Windows 7 and Vista only) and select the photos you want to fuse by ticking their boxes ❶. Start with two photos at the beginning. Click the Create tab ❷ and the Photo Fuse button ❸.

2 One of the faces in your photo will be selected for swapping ❶. You can move and enlarge this box using the handles ❷ – if the head has moved between shots, for example, select more of the body around it, or it may not fit properly. Select the version you prefer ❸.

3 Aim to get the body parts looking right (we'll fix areas of clothing in a minute). If you're reasonably happy with the results, click the Save button ❶, give the picture a new name ❷ and click Save again ❸.

4 If you need to, open the picture in an image editor – we've used Paint.net (www.getpaint.net). Zoom in on any sections that don't match up ❶. Clothes are easier to fix than body parts, which is why we enlarged the box area in Step 2.

5 Select a piece of clothing using the Rectangle, Lasso and Ellipse Select tools ❶. From the Selection Mode button, alternate between 'Add (union)' ❷ and Subtract ❸ until you're fairly close to getting the shape you need. Copy it using the keyboard shortcut Ctrl+C.

6 Paste the selection back into the image as a new layer (Ctrl+ Shift+V) and use the handles ❶ to stretch and distort the selection to fill any gaps. You can use multiple layers on top of one another to re-create the background and foreground. Save the image when it's done.

Can I customise Gmail to hide unwanted features?

http://bit.ly/minigmail263 ⏱ 5 mins

Gmail is loaded with features, but chances are you don't use all of them. Minimalist for Gmail is a Chrome add-on that removes ads and shows only the features you need.

It lets you change its appearance, and offers more options than the standard Gmail settings. A similar service is available for Firefox from http://mattconstantine.com/mg.

1 After installing the extension, click the envelope icon ❶ in the Chrome address bar to open the Minimalist Gmail options. Click Options ❷ and a new tab will open. Use the navigation bar on the left to open options on the right.

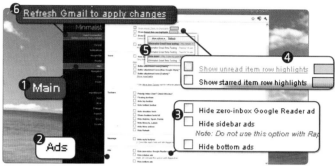

2 To hide ads, go to Main ❶, Ads ❷ and tick what you want to hide ❸. Here you can also hide toolbars and icons and colour-code emails ❹. Hover over an option to see a preview ❺. To save changes, click 'Refresh Gmail to apply changes' ❻.

3 For advanced layout options, go to Navigation ❶. Tick the boxes next to buttons, links or sections you don't use to hide each one individually, or hide all the toolbars by clicking 'Hide navigation' ❷. You can remove Chat in the Chat menu ❸. Save your changes.

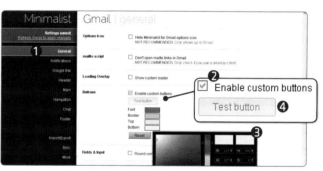

4 Once you've chosen your toolbars, you can change the design of the buttons in General ❶. Tick the box to 'Enable custom buttons' ❷, then click Font, Border, Top and Bottom and use the colour-picker ❸. The test button ❹ shows you a preview. Save your changes.

5 You can replace the Gmail logo with your own image by going to the Header menu ❶. In the Logo section ❷, click 'Enable custom logo' ❸. You'll need to host your image on an online image-sharing site then paste its URL into the box ❹. Alternatively, you can hide the logo completely.

6 If you have Gmail as a pinned tab in your browser, you can use Minimalist for Gmail to add a notification option to the favicon showing you how many new messages you've received ❶. Go to Notifications ❷ and click 'Enable favicon unread counter' ❸. Save your changes.

INSIDE THIS MONEY-SAVING GUIDE YOU'LL FIND...

362 WAYS YOU CAN SAVE MONEY!

33 PC & WEB WORKSHOPS!

255 FREE SOFTWARE DOWNLOADS!

53 PAGES OF PRACTICAL PC ADVICE!

PLUS...

22 SECRET TIPS FROM MARTIN LEWIS!